REVIEWS FOR:

Messages in Nature

In her book, *Messages in Nature*, Katy paints with words, a canvas of this earth's natural world. As a hiker, Katy can go to many places the average person cannot go. However, with her vivid portraits, it is easy to feel one's self walking along with her, experiencing endless crashing of waves against ragged cliffs, majestic towering mountains, eagles flying overhead in search of food, and wildflowers covering the earth's floor, leaving their scent for all who pass by.

But, more importantly, Katy paints a picture of the glorious Creator of this natural world that we love and enjoy. She points us to the Creator who longs to be with His creation, who shows the extent of His love with the promise, "I will never leave you nor forsake you."

—Helen Allen, Bible Teacher.

***

I loved this book! It is a must-read for all nature-loving and God-fearing believers. Katy brings to life each natural scene, painting a picture of how God intends us to view or feel it through His eyes and senses. Take a hike with her and experience our world in vivid heavenly frameworks.

—Nicole Kirchner.

i

***

I grew up in Maine and have had the joy of experiencing many of the moments that author Katy describes in her writing. I've been away from New England for several years, and, reading Katy's words has let me just close my eyes and relive those moments, as though I were there again!

Once the scene is set, she goes on to give all glory to the One who created the beauty and majesty she so aptly describes. In this stress-filled world, reading Katy's work allows one to set everything else aside and enter into peaceful fellowship with God, and to give Him glory and thanks for His wonderful works. I recommend this book!

—**Bette Johannes**.

***

It was a privilege to read excerpts from Katy Morris' book, *Messages in Nature*. Katy has a gift in writing that is rare. She so eloquently describes what she sees as well as what she feels through nature. It makes me feel as though I am experiencing nature with her, using all of my senses. Added to this, she capably connects the mental scene created by the Creator using beautiful and pertinent Biblical quotes.

I am anxiously awaiting to purchase a copy of her book for myself as well as for other people who I know will find it both enjoyable and uplifting.

—**Janet Kirkwood**, Retired RN.

Messages in Nature

K. J. Morris

Published by KHARIS PUBLISHING, imprint of KHARIS MEDIA LLC.

ISBN-13: 978-1-946277-91-6
ISBN-10: 1-946277-91-6

Library of Congress Control Number: 2021934345

All KHARIS PUBLISHING products are available at special quantity discounts for bulk purchase for sales promotions, premiums, fund-raising, and educational needs. For details, contact:

Kharis Media LLC
Tel: 1-479-599-8657
support@kharispublishing.com
www.kharispublishing.com

If you really want to know Him, you must give way to the internal drive that will lead you down the path to His world, raw, untouched nature. The craggy Maine coast and the remote northern wilderness. Nature in its natural state, unembellished by human hands; its full potential unleashed and radiating Him. The physical senses are only half the experience. No other place on earth embodies the Father of it all, so manifestly as His creation.

—Psalm 19:1-4a

"Messages in Nature" did not evolve from social realism, but draws heavily on the workings of nature, the whispers from rustling scrubs, the smudge of crags on the horizon, the soft music of the waters all awe-inspiring, and inadvertently culminating in passionate and uplifting messages. A reprieve from the hassles of daily life, each page sizzles with love and hope.

This book is a truth fiercely told, with a lovely and authentic linguistic lilt, and speaks to everyone regardless of their race, gender, background, or social stratum. There is a word in here for the grounded Christian and the newbie, people who have had a personal revelation of who God is and people looking to know him, naturalists and those indifferent – even oblivious – to the wonders of nature; through the eyes of the narrator, we experience firsthand the omnipresence of God, expressed in nature, and the interminable energy binding us all to Him.

Dedication

*To my parents, George & Shelley: For their support, their love, and their encouragement to attain the higher life....
that these words may relay it so.
To Walter and Diane: For their continuous enthusiasm for this book, and the anticipation that all readers come to know the Father through it.
And to Him: The Author and Finisher of our faith. May all accolades be rendered at His throne. Our only Hope, our Breath, our Reason to never give up.*

TABLE OF CONTENTS

Autumn in Appleton Ridge, Maine

Barter's Island, Maine

1

Cross Country Trip Awakens Pen

Pennsylvania, Delaware River—Strong Winter Nighttime Storm

Darkness, then sudden illuminating light, show-case the truth of the fiercely flowing river. Re-sounding surges of unleashed fury from other, unfa-miliar origins, dominate the flashes of light in perfect cadence. The thunderstorm is taking dominion and boasting its full array of power. It has taken control over the area, *overriding the natural order* of the tim-ing of the season.

Do you know what I have given unto you, My Chil-dren? Remember, back in the beginning of time, when I gave man dominion over the earth and all the creatures that inhabited it? This is still yours! It is your right to rule over all things on earth and under Heaven in My name. So, I tell you, do not be afraid when you experience all sorts of magnificent displays of terror on the earth. These things will happen and come to pass. I have called you to go into the fire and lion's den, as did Daniel.

I have told you that you will walk through the valley of the shadow of death. These are astonishing commands utilizing only man's power. A thousand may lay at your side and ten thousand on your right. ***But never forget*** you are in the shelter of the Most-High. I am subject to NOTHING! Just as a prince holds the same protection and enjoys the inheritance of his father, the king, you also enjoy the covering of My wing.

Niagara Falls & Surrounding City

In the midst of this surrounding city, there springs up blue life, wildflowers, on the patches of non-existent front lawns. It is I!

The sound of the crashing falls rings out My declaration over this area: I am here! I am here, and I love these people!

North Dakota and Minnesota

These seemingly endless stretches of land and experiences are a glimpse for you into My viewpoint. There are no boundaries, limitations, or ends to My ever-expanding plans and routes. Anything you see is only a mirage; it is an illusion in My master design. I make a way where there is none. You see, I AM THE WAY,

I AM THE TRUTH, AND I AM THE LIFE. I laugh at the cankerworm which, in its oblivion, only burrows a bigger route for My illumination to manifest more brightly. I am the Way Maker.

Yellowstone Lake—Morning Awakens

The fog you see settling over the morning lake is as My breath beckoning the Life Force into every living thing.

Although in the night it became as though dead, I now breathe My Breath of Life onto the waters. And I say, come alive and let your beauty resemble My beauty.

3

This morning's view is a peephole into My persona. I am Life. In this next life, you will understand reality. There will be no more night, only morning!

My nature will permeate such a life force that NOTHING will exist except life, and life more abundantly.

Mount Washburn

These vast mountain ranges are merely a series of small hills compared to My never-ending Kingdom!

Though now you can hardly believe your eyes, what you are looking at does have an end. Eyes have not seen, ears have not heard, what I have prepared for my people. Only the best have I prepared; My finest banquets, My finest homes, and My finest displays mirror the deepest wishes in the recesses of your hearts.

My people will rule and reign. You will not be my subjects. You are My bloodline, My first passion. Come to Me now, while your eternity can still be secured.

Nothing in this earthly realm is weighty enough to compare with My invitation.

Old Faithful Geyser

Old Faithful.
Just as the name states,
I will be faithful to My people.
Be careful; do not grow weary in well-doing or wait-
ing.
I am coming for My people.
Watch! The signs are all around you, just as Old
Faithful gives its warning eruptions, gearing up for
the finale.
I am coming for those who are waiting and watching
in anticipation, never taking their eyes off the prize,
not looking to the left or right.
Only those faces which are set as flint, in a forward
gaze, will win the ultimate Prize—ME!
This age is swiftly coming to an end; reality will be
the only way forevermore.

Yellowstone, Lower Falls

Traversing this path is like traversing life's path. One must be determined and set in their mind to finish. Without this affirmation, fueled by love for Me, no one can attain this goal. The path will be exceedingly steep at times, and you can easily slip on the terrain if you do not keep your focus.

Solitude may press in on you, but you *must* trudge on, *for there is no other way leading to Life.* I will give you the ability to continue, if you lean on Me. Yes, I will provide respite for you along the way—those with like hearts and beautiful experiences. You may rest at these times, but be careful not to stop so long that you lose your focus. Many will become too entangled and will ultimately be blind to the path. They will believe they are living life to the fullest. Little do they realize they have sold their souls to this world; they have given up their birthright for a bowl of soup. Compared to what I offer, this soup is a cesspool!

Each person must walk this path with Me. Great friends and family can be an encouragement, but if you are leaning too hard on them, eventually you will be misguided.

I am your true Compass. Look nowhere else except Me for the fulfillment of every answer and crevice in your being.

Colorado Caves

I am the Light for your path.

You cannot traverse the way without My light, just as you cannot traverse the way in the caves without your lantern.

Alone, you have no idea what lies in the path ahead of you.

You must keep your lantern burning, for the longer your light goes out, the more lost you will become.

Those who refuse My light for a long span of time will eventually go blind.

Follow Me, the Bright Morning Star.

Nashville Hall of Fame

What is your measure of success?
The measure from Heaven, the eternal lens, is entirely opposite from earth's measure.
On earth, those who are "reaching for the stars" will attain nothing by My eternal standard.
Living for self, they have sold their souls for what this fallen world has to offer.
It is all a mirage, a lure that will never satisfy the desires behind their drives.
Those who have chosen Me, who are sold out to Me, will be My stars of Heaven for all of eternity

Northeast Tennessee - White Opening in Storm Sky Revealing Rainbow

As you go into the storm, know I oversee it. I surround you, as the rainbow fearlessly showcases its beauty during this storm. Rest like a sleeping baby in a mother's arms, knowing I have shielded you; your best interest is My specialty. The white opening amidst the steel-colored, foreboding clouds is the way I will bring you through.

Go through, My Child, and pay no attention to the dark clouds.

2

New England Nature Retreat

Northwestern Massachusetts—Stone Rock at Nature Retreat

I am the eternal Rock of Ages. I support you and I always go with you. You must only always make sure to come back to a place of alignment with Me. Be ever conscious of Me. By doing this, you will be upon Me, a solid foundation. Just as you now feel the impenetrable, immovable support for your body beneath you, such am I, *Lover of your soul*.

I am the Stone the builders rejected. Many have tried to build magnificent empires on earth, only to walk away with the same experience—utterly void of fulfillment and radiating longing, their foundations remaining amiss. With Me, you shall want for nothing.

I fill the chasms and crevices in you, as water fills the bottom of a rocky stream. I extend far beyond the experience of human love or loyalty; I encompass love with no beginning, no bounds, nor ending. I radiate love because I am Love. My people are My magnificent obsession, My outlet for My all-consuming drive. Come to Me for this infusion of Life.

Northwestern Massachusetts—Message of the Wind for the Weary Traveler

As I begin to breathe My breath of Life over every inch of this land, touching every detail, *so I desire to breathe into you.* The wind carries with it My longings to know My people more intimately. Many have learned to dread the coming rain, but the rain brings growth. Without the rainy season, your growth would be severely inhibited, eventually leading to death. Without rain, the flower turns inward, focusing solely on its own lack. It begins wilting and finally crumbles to its own demise.

This is not why I have created you. I made you to have the beauty of the flower that displays a new dance to the weary traveler, encouraging him in a silent, yet profound awakening. The traveler then opens his eyes to the coming sunlight after the storm. Life will bring you through times of intense pressure and questioning, you can easily become disillusioned.

The raindrops can blur your vision, unlike My intent of cleaning the debris from your eyes. You can become dangerously despondent, to the point of grief. Your path in life may not lead you in the way you foresaw, but this is alright. You do not have to live in regret, even if you believe you have made a mistake. Stop these thoughts. Stand erect. Allow the rain to cleanse your vision.

Follow Me because I turn **tragedy** into **triumph**. Your most damning mistakes appear that way only because your focus is on your perceived failure. Again, I say stop! Allow the wind to usher you to the path I am paving. I make all things brilliant. Do you not see? Any mistakes you make are simply a means for My creativity to showcase even greater outcomes!

Your weakness and your regrets are no match for My artistry. I am the One who calls into life those things that are dead. I am the One who creates something out of nothing.

The twinkle in My eye, the nod of My head, the twitch of My hand causes all barriers to disappear and release those sealed, chained locks upon steel doors. Surely your stumbles are not above Me! So do not dread the coming rains. Learn to welcome the rain as equally as the sun, knowing I am instilling a greater degree of tenacity within you for your future exploits. Problems and failures are only perceived illusions. I bring victory and new hope in every situation. *Remember the robust flower after a period of rain.*

Northwestern Massachusetts - Times of Solitude

I give My invitation for this time to release you from the pressures of life in which you remain so locked. I am here to help guide you and provide the best insurance for your well-being. Miss out on other things in life, but do not reject My invitation to connect with Me. Only in times of solitude can you become grafted and bonded to Me.

Hear My voice, heed My invitation. I call you to come away with Me for refreshment. The cooing doves in the morning are My beckoning to you. Such is the wind swirling around your body and the sunlight warming your skin. My insects of song, crickets, and grasshoppers, all in harmony, gently request your attention. Even the rain's melodious droplets cause you to stop and take notice. It is Me, inviting you into My table of communion. All of nature is voicing My deepest desire. This is My artistry, My way of bringing you into *a moment with Me.*

New Hampshire, White Mountains

As the clouds now envelop the mountains, I too wrap My arms around My people. You are not out of My reach. I hold you and cradle you with My profound presence. My sweet blanket is a comfort to the heart-wounded and to those whose hopes have been smashed.

Do not despair, My Child, My love for you is eternal. You will walk hand-in-hand with Me in My kingdom of joy and pleasure upon pleasure. Do not look at the present, for I have a future for you that out-reaches any earthly mountain. They are but a drop in the bucket comparted to your future. Rest in My cloud of safety.

Western Maine

Just as the light filters through the branches of the birches, so My arms reach to guide you. Follow the light to My path for you. *The road less taken is the one that will lead you to My otherwise unknown revelations.* Just as there is more revelation from the light on the other side of the birches, so is the walk in this lighted life with Me. Come on the other side. Follow the light. My arms are open wide. Come into My splendor, My magnificence. Come and be awed, My Child. Step into another realm and be attached to Me, like the birch branches clinging to their deeply rooted trunk.

Bethel, Maine—Spotlight of Sun on Cornfield

A great company, a great company; yes, they will be greater and more brilliant than these vibrantly erect cornstalks. My people will be My mighty brigade in unison. They will be decked and shielded with a heavenly husk, protected from the elements. They will be straight as arrows, no longer just having a form of godliness, for they will **become** it.

I am beckoning My army, calling them to reach for Me as intently as the corn reaches for the sun in this field. Indeed, My presence will be as the sun to this field. Unlike this corn, however, which is harvested for fleshly indulgence, My people will be the harvesters **bestowing life.**

Paris, Maine—Full Moon Evening

As the sun exits the horizon, all nature takes notice; looking and waiting for Me to pour Myself out as the dew. The trees become still, the crickets relay the message that I am coming for nighttime revelations! You need Me now in this dark time and I will impart My message. I will be walking, shining My Way through the night. Those who choose the worldly pleasures at this time will not notice Me in their indulgences. I shine like the moon, yet they don't notice Me. Be still and focus your eyes on My movement. It is not glittery, loud, or embellished with the eye candy of urban night life. I walk the narrow path that is less tantalizing, yet My path leads to life. All other paths, with their glamor, will lead to the unexpected end, the graveyard's trap.

3

Silent Words in a Child's Eyes

Waterville, Maine

I saw God's eyes today, as she rounded the corner with a carefree step; unassuming and free of worry, pain, or concern. These burdens were simply foreign and unbeknownst to her.

Her radiant brown eyes met mine, and immediately, without a word, she welcomed me into her world that was free from the chains of assumption and reservation. Those eyes transmitted a light of acceptance towards me. She motioned goodbye with a gesture, as best as her chubby little hand would allow. A brilliant smile, then she was gone.

I welcome everyone as this little child welcomed you. I don't look at your mistakes, lifestyle, class, career, or even attitude, as some believe. In this moment, I bid you to COME, bring ALL of you to Me, your faults, your shame, your barren places, perceived weaknesses, and strengths. Be with Me just as you are.

4

Rural Maine Life

Rockland, Maine—Fragrance of the Ocean

The waves are ever depositing their gift of shells upon the shoreline. My breath blows the gentlest breeze, ushering the ocean's aroma throughout the inland areas and My presence is infiltrating, like the salt in the air.

Have you been living on the coast so long that you bypass and no longer notice My aroma? Or perhaps you are new to this area, and are as enthralled with My mighty coastline as a child in a candy store.

When it comes to My presence, neither of these reactions are My ultimate for you. I desire for you to start your morning with a warm gladness that spreads over your heart, this being your internal clock, and easing your eyes open from nighttime sleep. My salt in the air is an instant revival to your being that no cup of coffee could ever accomplish.

I want us to be DEAR, OLD trusted friends, having the closeness of SOULMATES, with the STRENGTH of two seasoned, victorious veterans of war. I want the reason, the debut for your eyes opening each day, to be with Me.

Rockland, Maine—Coastal Maine Message

Now is the season that draws people from all over the globe to see My magnificent Maine coastline. The sun is shining down its warmth, heating those under it to blissful glee. They enjoy their fine food and pleasures that the riches of this world buy them. Today, Maine truly is vacationland. The difference five months from now, in the middle of winter, will be so stark a contrast. Then, many of the little, alluring shops will be locked behind sturdy doors; they will remain unvisited until late spring.

Doors that are now opened, or are of lightweight material, will be missing. Even the pathway to get to the few open shops will be wracked with hard ice and patches of compacted snow, making any step or standing uncertain. The snowbanks will compete with the height of each person. The coastline will send a bitter dare to those to come closer, for the heated sand will be gone, replaced with snowy spots and a stiff, penetrating wind. All will appear as a ghost town in comparison to today's carefree scene.

Who will go into this territory for Me? Who will deny themselves and put Me above their flesh? Who will love not their own body for My advancing kingdom? There are many, many barren places in the earth today. Some are deceiving, though they appear to flourish with every desire of man fulfilled. They may tantalize the eye, but from eternity's viewpoint, truly they are some of the poorest places. Fattened upon the pampering of the flesh, they will be found wanting and void of any true reserves on the day of accounting. My people are not on earth to be concerned with their own pleasures.

No, I need harvesters who are sold out to Me, saving these lost souls in the midst of their poverty. I will become the coastal summer day to anyone following Me! To you, I will be this experience that never ends, even though the worldly one does. I will be your gleaming summer sun as you walk into the iciest realms of the earth!

Owl's Head, Maine—True Grit

Everything in this rugged environment boasts of its true character. This is not a comfortable, sandy shore, but one that is rock-covered. These rocks compete with the huge, jagged ones that pepper the coastal water's edge.

Here you can lose your footing easily.

Large areas of the rocks are covered in wet seaweed. Barnacles line other rocks, providing good grip to the hiker, but also threatening a more painful ending to a fall than the softer seaweed. Brilliant, bright orange rosehips proudly showcase their color and tenacity, growing on vibrant, green bushes of impressive heights.

One, in a moment of awe, deciding to pick a rosehip, is quickly reminded of the pain-inflicting thorns guarding their beauty. The great cliffs, with their steep, rocky heights stand the test of time, through gentle fall days to fitful winter rages.

The seagull is a bird despised by some, but one from which you can learn. He navigates his environment effortlessly. He rides the incoming waves without worry; he does not fight them. He does so in such a fashion, creating the illusion that imminent danger is far away. So, too, are My tried-and-true soldiers, ever standing for the truth, no matter what is stirring across the waters. They are grounded by their love for Me; their very reason for existence is sold out devotion as a determined sacrifice of honor to Me. Yes, life here is a replica of My saints' lives, making My heart brim over with a Father's pride.

Rockland, Maine—Chickawaukie Pond

In their large flock, ducks find themselves enjoying a late afternoon bask in the sunlight. The heat of the day has faded. A delightful breeze lingers over the calm bay waters, playing host to the advancing, quiet evening. In their prime, beautiful birch trees line the humble landing. Mountains of thick trees are the canvas behind the water, pulling together the serene scene. All the ducks have the same shades of brown and gray feathers. His bright orange legs appear as a duck adjusts his position and burrows for a hidden treat on the grassy bank. Despite a "quack" heard here and there, it is an otherwise peaceful, content group. Then, amid the group, a seagull camouflaged in the same colors shows himself. He had blended in expertly, but now, seeing his form, it is obvious he is not one of them. Unable to deny his identity or become part of the group, he finds another lone seagull and makes his way there.

My children, so you, too, are not of this world. Live peacefully alongside those who do not know Me. Offer your love, a result of Me in you, as an outpouring for others. Do not BECOME them, but do ASSOCIATE with them, leading them to Me. You are My gateway for them. Keep your heart burning for Me, so you do not become lost in their maze. Be the map that leads them to Me.

Washington, Maine –For Those who Know of Me, but Don't Know Me

I create the most alluring invitations for people to commune with Me. Open your eyes beyond your circumstances. Is your life everything you had hoped it would be? If yes, then you are missing out, because I make life exceedingly and abundantly beyond what you have ever wanted or hoped for.

Is your life mediocre? Come, experience my Oil of Gladness that never dissipates. Is your life full of pain and collapsed dreams? I have the remedy for you, too, because I make all things new. Again, I say, OPEN

your EYES and accept My invitation. I AM THE AN-
SWER for every person.

You are surrounded now by My massive oak trees,
quietly overseeing you as I always do. Yes, the oaks
are like Me, steady, strong, and able to weather all
conditions. The temperature today? Isn't it perfec-
tion? That was for you, also. I lure you with the color
of the wildflowers swaying and inviting you to learn
their dance of freedom. I even ushered in the deer,
the whole herd, to wander into the meadow the exact
time I knew you would be here. I'm gently nudging
you, showcasing all of My artistry, enticing you, prov-
ing to you that you are indeed my first love.

Today, everything resembles Me in full blown life.
The trees are dressed in shades of their finest peak
green. The birds provide melodies for the soul. It's all
part of My marvelous set up. It was all done by My
hand for you, not in an historical and distant way as
when I first created the earth.

Nature did not simply evolve on its own from
there. No, it has been by My present hand, actively
guiding all My creation to lure you into My arms. *I
will be to you as your very backbone.* I will mold Myself as a sweet balm into all of your being. You will
never lack again, even in the areas you never knew
were empty.

Maine—Summer of the Perennials

The season has been exceedingly dry with drought-
like conditions. Only certain flowers, my hearty perennials, have stood the extreme conditions. The annuals are only alive because someone else has been
watering and feeding them for their survival. This is

not how I want My Children to be on life's journey. If you are rooted in Me, then you will be able to stand on your own. You will not succumb to the pressure, wilt, and die.

A severe drought is in today's society. Mankind has pushed Me and My order of decency and morality; yes, My very Spirit, OUT of their lives. It is no longer "appropriate" for Me to be in their government, schools, recreation, or even churches. Entire communities are CLEARLY in a state of war and, out of their own arrogance, remain blind to their ownership of the head-on slaughtering. The chaos and evil have come on the nightly news as continuous, sickening stories that people of past generations could never have even listened to. Society has gone so far that "entertainment" series are made of such storylines. Who could stand for Me in such sewage? But then I see My perennials, My little lights of color covering the earth today.

How I admire you. How I love you because you are My deep, clean, refreshing wells in this drought. The beauty of the annuals may be viewed as more magnificent than My perennials because they are adored by many, and placed in the center of attention. They enjoy the foremost happenings in life, they are directly in the middle of all the entertainment. They are pampered, even hand fed. My perennials, though, are in the background, many times not tended at all. They go unnoticed, viewed even as weeds, but they give the best gifts. Some of My most potent medicines in the plant kingdom comes from these, My herbs. My herbs can withstand rocky and dry conditions and some, to My heart's admonishment, have even learned to thrive there.

I speak to My beloved perennials now. I love you with a never-ending love. I cherish your sacrifice. You are My heart song. I see all the times, every single time, you have endured for Me and Me alone. I've watched the brutal sun scorch you with the unrelenting heat of the desert. I have seen your petals wilt in the ruthless afternoon hours.

But My dear ones, I have also seen you spring up, spring up, spring up the next morning, having been drinking only My dew to survive. I do not view this as shortcomings and failures. No, My beautiful ones, this is a testament to Me; these are My sold-out loyal ones, laying down their very lives in the face of death, and **choosing** to remain faithful to Me. By My blood coursing through you, and your testimony, you have overcome the evil one.

Yes, My dear ones, you are victorious in this precursor period, the time of choice between now and your eternal home. You have overcome the evil one and still stand! Be of cheer, not downtrodden, for the beauty and accolades of the annuals are fleeting. You have chosen to be perennials that last for eternity. YOU will be MY MOST CELEBRATED flowers in My Kingdom forevermore.

Fairfield, Maine—The Thrill of Me

I am the Calm before the storm. I am the Shelter during the storm. I am the Rainbow after the storm. I am the Good Shepherd that ALWAYS saves the one, lost sheep. I initiate the dawn and give My release for the dusk. I ordain gifts for both the grateful and ungrateful. I hear the cries of the desperate, deafened by deep layers of pain to others. The cry goes unrecognized and is drowned in a sea of noises and distractions. But to Me it is as clear as that of a mother immediately knowing the unique sound of her baby's plea.

With a battered and broken body, I carried the cross. Abused, despised, and humiliated, I endured for the very ones who nailed me to it. I chose the twelve disciples when I knew they would all walk away from Me, after seeing miracles and experiencing My true love. In My darkest, most agonizing hours, I knew they would fall asleep, eventually denying Me and scattering, thus causing the human condition of isolation and rejection to radiate within Me. Through all this, My love continually abounds and spills over from Me for all people. *This is the thrill of knowing Me.*

Benton, Maine—Before the Rain

Do you see the signs of the coming rain? It is My rain of refreshment. Be content today, knowing I come to blanket this area in peace.

The wind is gently moving throughout. The trees sway. There begins the quiet lull, then My gift comes down upon the earth from the heavens.

My intention is for you to stop today. You weary souls, come to Me to be revived, as parched flowers. Forget all else, focus on Me alone. Allow your body to relax and release all unnecessary tension. Feel the cleansing peace coming down, washing away the inhibiting debris.

Allow Me into your whole being and experience a soundness that exists only by Me within you.

Stockton Springs, Maine Bay—Doorway to Reality

This spot on earth is off the beaten path. The only trail entering is hidden from the few visitors to this area. Many visitors seek finer attractions and never come to this area at all, let alone to this spot. If you look for it with all your heart, you will find it. Do not follow the crowd and miss out by passing the trail opening. In doing so, you would also miss out on Me today. This path leads to My voice; the paved way leads to the noisy voices of man. They drown out what I offer at the end of the hidden trail.

Regular visitors are not found on this hidden part of the bay. There are no convenient amenities here. I ask you to rest and listen to the hidden messages behind the sounds of swaying wind, occasional bird calls, and the silence of your inner thoughts. Walk along the shore. Examine My remains upon the sandy and rocky ground as I pull back the waters. Enter My dimension, the dimension that is reality. This bay is the entrance to that place if you quietly welcome Me to engage with you.

Do not look for a lightning bolt, or a shock of Me making Myself known to you. I will not meet you in that manner here. If you are looking for that, you are not truly looking for Me. This place is also not meant as somewhere for you to become lazy and fall asleep. This is a quiet, elusive place that could cause you to do that, but I have placed this bay here on earth for people to become refreshed and awakened to My reality. This bay is an open doorway. It offers the ability for all who walk here to become enlightened to the secrets in My kingdom and in My true Self.

I will surpass the boundaries in your mind and what you know as the "laws of nature." The real world does not work according to these principles. The real world is the one we share together as you walk with Me. This is when your old reality becomes new. It becomes the accurate reality, the ONLY one in your life. Come down this path, into this bay, and enter in. Without Me, your reality alone is a mere prison sentence of time.

Washington, Maine—Warning in the Green Grass

Many possess the cunning to blend into My church, appearing to be something they are not. Anyone can be fooled quite easily into believing these are My followers, as they expertly wear their "camouflage." They are so skilled in their act that they deceive everyone in their paths who are without My guidance. Some of these deceivers blend in so well that they have lost sight of their true condition, thus fulfilling the scripture of the mirror [James 1: 23-25]. These are the *preying* mantises among My true believers, much like the praying mantis in the blades of grass at your feet.

He lays in wait, his front legs upward in a prayer-like position, however, he is *not* seeking to pray, but seeking prey. Those who are not fine-tuned to My voice will become their prey. Beware, My Children! Beware! He is waiting to devour the next victim who comes too close. Yes, I know you assumed he was another blade of grass. In fact, you were totally oblivious to his presence, due to his ability to conform to his surroundings.

Then your eyes became focused with an eagle's sight—that was Me—causing you to see with x-ray vision. I inhabit your eyes because you have given Me your being; thus you were able to detect the real grass from the masterfully disguised insect. *You will know them who truly love Me, because their entire lifestyle will be consumed with keeping My commandments,* just like a child eager to please his father. With true love, it is not burdensome, but a pleasure.

In Me, you live, move, and have your being! Although the mantis goes through the motions of a believer, he is not! Be on guard for him, for he is an instrument for the devouring lion. Be not deceived by his appearance, for he will quickly consume you. This is not a light warning I give you. Do not judge a person by their outward stance, or words and philosophies. These are the ones who, although they **appear** enlightened, are actually **darkened** and have become the fools of this world. Their hearts' intentions are to destroy My kingdom.

Do not take My warning frivolously. Those who are not sold out to Me are destroying My church. Ultimately, they do NOT want My will. **When the telltale time of choosing is at hand,** *they choose their own will*. This is the spirit of antichrist. It is packaged very alluringly to the eye of man. It seems *very* good, but IT IS NOT ME! They are not of Me!

Do not associate with or give your pearls to these dogs, these wolves in sheep's clothing. This is My warning to you, wrapped in My love of protection. The mantis will bring down whomever chooses to walk closely with him. Keep your eyes in tune with Mine, for I know the hearts of man, and I will never steer you to be devoured. You will remain safe if you walk with Me, obeying My commandments. You will be in the unconquerable shelter of the Most High!

5

A Month along Togus Pond

Augusta, Maine, Togus Pond

I am the rare gem along the shoreline. I am the prize for those who choose to run the race. A runner in a race is not someone taking a casual stroll, he is the extreme opposite. He has made himself go through rigorous training, denying the comforts for which his body aches. He pushes himself with all his might. His complete focus is on the race. He is not looking to the left or right. His gaze is straight ahead and his body is offering every ounce of strength it can muster. His mind has but one focus. He is determined to run and win because to him, there are no other options.

This is how I call you to partake in this race of life, with full-time devotion. The impending weather or time of day do not matter to the runner; he trains in rain and remains devoted – be it Friday night or Sunday morning. Serving Me is not a matter of timing or convenience. For you to win, I must be your greatest passion, your reason for living.

Without Me, you could not bear the thought of living. There is nothing to be compared with the winner's Prize for those who are truly in this race. I am the Prize! Those who stroll in a race are not worthy to partake in the honor; they are disqualified for such apathy. How is it then, that anyone believes the race leading to eternal life should be for those who choose comfort, and have a blatant disregard of My rules? My marvelous racers are those who have predetermined to stay the course until they hear My words, of which they have dreamt so often: "Well done thou good and faithful servant... enter thou into the joy of thy Lord." [Matthew 25:21]

Augusta, Maine, Togus Pond Evening—Be with Me

As the summer comes to a close, the subtleties of fall are around. Tonight, though, I bring you a pleasant, spring-like evening; it is so close to the aura of spring that one could easily believe it is so. I cause the sun to warm your body through the dancing pendulum of hemlock branches, their glory reflecting on the waters below. Lilly pads showcase their vibrant color under the gleam. I breathe down upon you now, and time itself is powerless, frozen in the moment.

The birds coming forth bring an undeniably springtime song, the flowers gleam in mesmerizing rainbow shades. A soft carpet of pine needles covers the bank, encouraging all to come to the water's edge. I am the One who brings this spring-like day to you now, to all who want My refreshment. All of this ushers in My presence, leading you to Me. Just as special as a man planning the setting for a proposal of a lifetime together, so I request you. I am the King of Kings, robed in honor and power, always Faithful, always True, the Lover of your soul, a Friend like no other. I AM the guarantee amidst all uncertainty. Yes, this is My Grand Opening, My Grand Entrance. You are on My guest list. Won't you enter in?

Augusta, Maine, Togus Pond

I am the Crowning Touch on the hemlocks. The glisten of the light from above touches their gently swaying, green décor moving from the Life force in Me. The hemlock is a shadowy and mysterious tree. In groups it will cause any area to succumb to a cast of darkness. But when I shine My light on the hemlock, it illuminates into a brilliant green, expelling the darkness, *completely changing a setting from uncertainty to hope.* Such is this life pertaining to Me! Light turns the scene from a black forest to a dazzling array of emerald green.

The greatest chasm of darkness is always overtaken with any minuscule ray of My light. As for Me, I come into the darkness and it immediately dispels, losing its grip. As a lion who has lost his battle and retreats back into his cave, he has now transformed from a **threat** to a **victory**.

I MAKE THE VERY DARKNESS A SONG OF TRI-UMPH FOR YOU! You become a conqueror, so DO NOT fear the darkness. Only and always look for the light. I am forever shining the way with the light for you. Because I AM THE WAY and I AM THE LIGHT!

Augusta, Maine, Togus Pond—Diamonds on the Water

Sparkling diamonds shine on the surface of the water, playing tribute as an earthly replica of Me. The scene is dazzling, too bright to stare at. The birch trees are highlighted with waving leaves. A bird echoes its song over the sound-enhancing platform of the pond. It is the opening stage of My performance for all to partake. Mine is a creation no artist could capture, a masterpiece causing cold hearts to soften, disillusioned minds to awaken, and sick bodies to dance. The FREE show this evening is titled, "My Breath of Life."

Augusta, Maine, Togus Pond—A Fine Mist

A soft mist from Heaven deposits onto the tiny patch on the earth. The gentle gift lulls all movement. It is not a downpour that scatters the life, but a soothing layer of tranquility and purity overtaking the environment. The winged creatures of music go from full-blown song to murmur. The mighty pines and hemlocks stand motionless as the liquid highlights their green coats of honor. The clouds form grey snowballs, accented with brilliant white edges. Everything holds its breath for reprieve all of nature waits for the Presence to sweep and saturate. Then He is here,

31

enmeshed in the air. The mist lightens; the sun over-powers.

Who has waited here to commune with Me? I know many have fallen in despair. I see this earth has become a battleground even for My most decorated warriors. I have felt the groans coming from your chests, the longing for all things to be made new, pure and wholesome, void of fear. I give you a touch of this now to help you on your journey toward the doorway of Heaven.

There are other doors at which you can find yourself at the end of this life. There is only one path that will lead you to the Doorway of Delight. Any experiences of satisfaction on earth will be a dismal, mundane boredom in comparison to this threshold. This is when you come to fully experience life. Nothing on earth can compare.

Flowers never fade. Sweet symphonies never end. Vibrant life is in everything. Death is completely obliterated. My Child, do you not realize that a shadow cannot even exist in My full-blown Presence? It is pure Light. Nothing will have mattered concerning your journey, except that we were BEST friends. This is because I AM YOUR CALLING. Your work is fulfilled when we are in close relationship and you are yielding to My voice. I am here for all those who want TRUE success in this fleeting opportunity on earth. I AM YOUR OPPORTUNITY! Nothing else matters except being linked with Me, Maker of the heavens and earth!

Augusta, Maine, Togus Pond—Diving Hawk

The splash can be heard across the pond again and again. Quickly and fiercely, the eye of the predator is looking for the fish playing on the surface. The closer the fish is to the predator's world, the closer he is to death.

Many today are playing on the surface, desiring My blessings and eternal security, but a love of the world has caused them to linger and not fully immerse themselves. On the surface they believe the illusion that they are safe. This is not reality. They are merely fulfilling the scripture of enjoying their sin for a season. They are in a condition of apathy, causing their deception.

This is such a dangerous state to be in. You see, you can easily be pulled into the world, caught in the hawk's mouth in an instant. You must be deep in the water, sold out to Me. You must jump in with your WHOLE body, not just wade in foot-deep or knee-deep. You must be fully immersed in Me, totally surrendered. Nobody will conquer this course whose heart is divided between two masters.

Augusta, Maine, Togus Pond

The day becomes warmer, creating the illusion that this will be as any other day; the sun will emerge and any possibility of a rainstorm will be far from the concern of man. The heat builds and the day progresses. Man goes about his business. The pull of demands has totally occupied his mind. The pressure from other sources dull his awareness. Then the clouds quietly, slowly begin to overtake the sky. The creatures, seeing the signs, scamper for cover.

The air is heavy with only a gentle movement, having the ability to lull one to sleep with its incantation. The birds hush. The perception is that all is normal and will continue, as it has day after day, month after month, year after year. But then the tree leaves bend and turn upward, the clouds reveal one small, blue opening in the sky. The mounting signs are all around.

Will you be ready for the commencement of My unrelenting Kingdom? Man believes he has time; he will wait and make everything right when the signs of the end are upon him. But I tell you THE SIGNS ARE HERE. As a bow being stretched to its limit and the arrow releasing, so will My coming be. Man's ears are dull and his eyes have dimmed in apathy. This is no condition to be in, prior to My return. These are truly the five virgins who have grown lax in waiting and their lights have gone out. Man will beg for a second chance, but I have forewarned you that there is no second chance. You will have no time for repentance, you must be ready now. This is why My coming has been described as a "thief in the night," "a blink of the eye," and "lightning flashing from east to west." This is how quickly I will come! In an instant!

Do not strive for the comforts of this world. Do not become preoccupied with the phrase, "You only live once." The only place you can truly fulfill this saying is with your life after earth. Now, your life is as the grass that fades. You are here today and gone tomorrow, but your life afterwards is ETERNAL. There is no second chance! Seize the day, TODAY, to live your life for the eternal and not the temporary. Be close to Me and never risk losing the most important aspect of your life on earth My return.

All your efforts for gratifying the flesh will be of no value in an instant. Truly the ones who have attained the great mansions, traveled to and fro all over the earth, and have acquired great riches, will be the ones weeping in sorrow on that day, presently unbeknownst only to man. Now is not the time for slumber before My great entrance. KEEP YOUR GAZE ON ME. I am coming, King of Kings and Lord of Lords, and of My Kingdom there will be no end! ⅃

Augusta, Maine, Togus Pond—Mirror Morning on Pond

Like a transparent sheet of ice is the pond this morning. Everything on land is a perfect mirror image of its reflection. Nothing is hidden, all is on display on the still water.

The world around you is the pond and you are MY reflection, which is as I want your life to be, with nothing hidden, only a life of truth, only My representation. The nature shown in the pond this morning is an image of My nature. I hide nothing; everything is in full view. I have no reason to hide anything because I am altogether lovely, true, genuine, pure, holy, spotless, and blameless. *My very name* is FAITHFUL AND TRUE! So is your life when hidden in Mine.

Others will look and gasp at your stamina. How can this person maintain such strength, such dignity, and an openly honest life that is free from hiding behind closed doors? How is this person so unlike the typical lifestyle that is void of any depth? Today, how is it that so many are hiding, even in My church? The answer is sin. People are hiding in the dark, creating a total illusion of fulfillment and happiness, when their lives are out of order and shameful to their very selves. Today, in this culture, the insatiable lust is to satisfy SELF *at any cost.* Parents have their children at stake, marriage unions crumble, blood relations are at war, *I am put aside.*

The unquenchable question of today's society is, "How can I please myself?" You are presently seeing the fulfillment of My Word: "People will be lovers of themselves." This is all accepted as right and good; it is all packaged as the modern-wrapped philosophy of "Being true to myself," but it is NOT right and good. The permeating stench of self's eternal effects is repulsive to Me. In reality, being true to self is selfishness. That is not the image I want portrayed on your pond. Follow Me and you will be a reflection of everything that is good and wholesome. Your image need never be hidden, if you are hidden in Me.

Augusta, Maine, Togus Pond

I show you My love in all I do. Nothing I do, nothing I am, falls outside this. Completely sacrificial and all-consuming is My desire for you. But it is not *just* desire, it is *willful action* on My part. I do not merely proclaim My love for you; *My being is so in tune with this love that it is part of My very identity.*

Nature is My art canvas for it. It is My love letter to you. It is My symphony orchestra, My theatrical display. It is My all-consuming mission to draw you—not force you—to Me. Anything less than your choice is not authentic. I want the genuine manifestation of love that overflows between us.

Augusta, Maine, Togus Pond Morning

A new wind picks up and swooshes through the land, leaving nothing the same. Suddenly, everything is pulsating and dancing. Life and acceleration have overtaken the quiet spot. The dark rain of last night is gone, bringing a new purity of scent in the air. The pines boast their resinous, cleansing aroma. Sharp and distinct, it is a revitalizing scent to even the weariest of minds. The waters flow softly, transporting the observer from darkness to enlightenment. "Good Morning" greetings are offered as the birds cheerily proclaim the time of day. All of nature mingles together in harmony on this new day.

This is My proclamation to you: It is a new day! Brush off the dust of yesterday. Brush it off and do not return to it! Do not mourn as you do this. Allow your heart to leap, allow joy to reside, and experience My hand in a Father's blessing. My arm is never too short to reach you. The most desperate state, when all else has failed, when everything has died, does not become an obstacle for Me! *Remember, I create a new way.* I am Creator of Heaven and earth.

The very morning is heralded by My command. I hold the earth in place and I live outside of time; I am ABOVE time itself! My Child, surely if time holds no power over Me, then I can recreate and restore the years the canker worm has stolen.

Don't feel the pain of yesterday and time already gone. I AM HERE TO RENEW AND RESTORE. Don't you know, I only make things better? I do not create trash or mediocrity; I create the finest and best, because I am the ORIGINAL CREATOR. I am the embodiment of creation. In fact, I never stop creating. MY abilities exceed those of any talent because I am the God Who *calls things to life, as though they were dead*! I am the God Who creates SOMETHING out of NOTHING. So, give your nothing to Me! **I will take you, your heart, and transform you into such a high frequency of life that each beat will bring a coursing of My blood through your life, leaving NOTHING untouched!** *I will create all of this for you out of the dust of your yesterday.*

Augusta, Maine, Togus Pond

Those who are in tune can feel fall advancing in the air. It has been a warm day; going by the temperature alone there would be no thought of fall. But do you sense the signs? Yes, that's an acorn dropping from the top of the oak. If one looks closely, they can see My telltale brush strokes of color on the first of the surrendering trees. The creatures are preparing their winter dwellings. Some flowers have stopped producing their summer displays. The apples are suspended in the trees, and although small, they are very present. The evening creeps in with cooler nights.

The signs of My return are also in the air. A stiff coldness in the hearts of mankind is on display. The weather patterns are changing and unpredictable.

The news is filled with proof of imminent wars. Pride in human achievement and haughtiness are found in the thoughts of man. Many believe they have found better and more enlightened ways of living their lives. What I have deemed wrong is worshipped as right.

This is My world I have created, yet I have been swept out of society; My ways are no longer viewed as useful or necessary. The family is not in unison, but each member looks to fulfill their own wants. My children are lulled as to the warmth from the last summer's days, believing humanistic deceptions. But I am coming, just as I have promised. My return will take place just as I have stated.

The fall leaves showcase their brilliance for a short period before dropping and being left behind to face the reality of winter. So, also, shall a great number of people be left behind to face the world's frightening chaos after My return. I call out **now**, to every man and woman willing to deny themselves and follow Me, the Great Shepherd, always in relentless search of My lost sheep.

Augusta, Maine, Arboretum

Experience the canopy of My love down this trail of pines. These pine trees reach out their branches and extend overhead into a ceiling of green that shields you from the day's sun. Walk down the carpet of pine needles and feel the cushion that effectively softens your step. You are sheltered in My canopy. This trail is a conduit of My embracing arms around you. This is how I operate in your life in the unseen realm.

I am your Strong Tower that covers you. I am softening the blows in life that may trip you. I am all around you, and in you, just like the cleansing pine air you inhale in this spot. The priceless peace on this trail is the same peace you can take with you as a constant in life. It is there for you to possess as simply as reaching out and grabbing the pine needles overhead. ✓

Augusta, Maine, Togus Pond Afternoon

There is a shifting in the air today as I usher forth the afternoon rains. It has been so very dry, My Child. I have seen the heat of the relentless season with NO RAIN. There has been no respite for the flesh, only My very presence to sustain life. Life wilts and dies without water, BUT I AM YOUR WELL THAT NEVER GOES DRY, even in the drought. I will never leave you, nor forsake you. I have promised it and I, Faithful and True, never go back on My promises!

This afternoon rain brings in a new forecast. The drought is losing its grip as the rains have begun. Look up! Straighten your shoulders and raise up your head. New life is coming with the rain. Can you smell the difference My rain is bringing? It is cleansing away stale air; my Breath of Life is moving in and blowing throughout every crevice. The parched, dusty ground immediately drinks in the moisture as life-giving medicine, just as My presence is to your being. I move in with the rains, during this season where there is nothing but stubble in sight. But you know, Child... WITH THE RAIN COMES LIFE AFTERWARDS! And so, I call it forth in the atmosphere as I call forth the very dawn.

I release you, RAINS, down onto the earth's face, that is now so dry it could kindle and flame from one more spark of affliction. **But I RAISE MY HAND AND I SAY, ENOUGH, ENOUGH drought!** *Now, my dear one, I release to you LIFE!*

Augusta, Maine, Togus Pond Trail

Nature is beginning to fall as the season embarks on its mission to fulfill its name. Everything that was so full of strength is loosening its firm grip. Acorns and leaves alike are starting to fall; the final fruits are also dropping from the trees. Animals fresh from the vigor of summer begin to retreat and succumb to the new season. The warm life in the water is cooling and slowing. The flowers are no longer in the peak of their beauty and the grass has gone from growing, bright, green blades to dull and stagnant shades.

Summer has lost its grip. The pressing heat of the day is gone. Although it seems life is dying around you, it is just the ruling season losing its power. The fall does bring change with it, and is now signaling the end of a heated oppression. The fall air has extinguished the stifling heat and its aroma imparts a refreshment for the ones who have been in the fiercest battles.

The tables are turning; the firm grip of the intense combat is ending. Summer is retreating. fall is bringing serenity and a time of peace. Step into the change. Don't dread the change; don't be worried about survival by asking how your needs shall be met during this season. Simply step onto the new trails. Though they look different in the change of season, rest assured they are leading you to new experiences and new insights. Just as the view will illuminate into a glorious display of color this fall, so, too, will your life change and be filled with breathtaking happenings.

Augusta, Maine, Togus Pond

In this life, you cannot put your hope in anything or anyone, or you will risk falling prey to the human condition of deep disappointment and heartache. Listen to Me, Child, and remember My lifesaving words. The seasons will change. People will change, not only due to their changing will at times, but also due to things outside their will. In other words, people can shift from hot to lukewarm and even to cold in their walk with Me. People's circumstances can change, causing them to start a new life elsewhere, or even to pass away from this present world. People can greatly disappoint you. If you have not safeguarded your heart with Me, these times can bring you into the dangerous state of disillusionment. At this moment, your heart can seize up and close itself to others in a desperate attempt to save you from further pain. You can also grow hard and callous. *If you feast upon this, you can lose your way completely, and endanger your eternity with Me.*

DO NOT place anyone or anything in the high regard of total loyalty to you. This life will bring ups and downs from all directions. This is how the path of life twists and turns. This life is not about what you can attain or accomplish in it. I am your ONLY ATTAINMENT, your ONLY ACCOMPLISHMENT. Always remember, you are NEVER to put your hope, trust, or plans upon the fleeting things of this world. Anything and anyone can be taken away in an instant. The only assured guarantee is Me. THERE IS NOBODY NOR ANYTHING that can be to you what I am—Constant.

Augusta, Maine, Togus Pond—Rainy Morning

My melody of Heaven is the soft raindrops hitting the earth and all that lies below. The melody in Heaven ushers in a cleansing and a NEWNESS every time. Just as music changes the atmosphere in an unseen way, so does this morning's melody. This atmospheric change is My presence manifested to you. You can feel the change, but you cannot see it with your physical eyes.

It is like this with love, joy, and peace. I am not talking about fleeting "feelings;" I am talking about the inner sense of your spirit being magnetized to Mine in *a joining of US* that brings with it these constant attributes, *not* mere "feelings." As you are drawn into Me, I begin to encompass your everything. Your perceptions will become accurate, your heart will be purified, your entire being will understand the true meaning of life and life more abundantly.

Like a well that never goes dry, I am constantly refilling you to overflowing. This overflowing of My rain is meant to spill over, for the spilling over is what touches others around you. Your burden of saving and delivering someone is gone. It is My yoke that is easy and produces a domino effect on all life forms around you.

Become silent at this moment, and now hear only My melody, the rain. Allow no other thought to come into your mind. Open yourself to Me. Be done with the worries of today and give Me that pressure. I will take your burden and turn you from a state of lacking into a beating of your heart coursing abundance through your system. Come away with Me and never look back! Make your choice now, to follow Me with all your heart, soul, and mind. To you, I will be more precious than the air you breathe. The love between us will be unlike anything you can ever experience with another!

Augusta, Maine, Togus Pond—Afternoon Clouded Sky

I bid you to come. I give you the invitation, the opportunity, not just of a lifetime, but of *eternity's security.* My love is so great that a lifetime could never contain it. Like a thick blanket, the clouds cover the entire sky today. My love also envelops all; it has no holes. You cannot exhaust My desire for you. I am relentless in My pursuit of you, the object of My attention, the apple of My eye. I delight in just being with you. You need not entertain or flatter Me, as you might someone in your human relationships. There is never a need to re-invent "the flame," because My passion for you is the same magnitude as it was on the day, I created you. More accurately, it is as it was before time, even before you were born on this earth.

You see Child, My love is not human love, which is based on conditions and parameters. MY LOVE HAS NO FORM OF SELF IN IT. *I know you cannot even begin to conceive of My all-encompassing love.* If you look for fulfillment in other areas, a respected career, a lucrative life, exotic locations, man-made attempts for security, a soulmate with whom to live out your life... ANYTHING, My Child, *other than Me,* will leave you an empty and decaying shell in light of My love.

Yes, some of these things are nice and even beneficial for you, but understand, when they replace Me, they give only an unexpected emptiness in return.

I created the human soul to be tied first and only to Me. *I created places in you that only come alive with vibrant health and wholeness when I am your first Love.* There are areas in you that only I know. If I am the only One to know of these places, Child, then how can any other measure possibly fill them? I know the very best for each of My unique children.

You are My masterpieces, My finest works; you are the only part of My creation that is made in My image. Stand tall and love Me with all your being. Pursue Me with all your might. In return, I will give you My most precious and valuable assets for your inheritance.

Augusta, Maine, Togus Pond Afternoon

The tree branches do not resist the moving of the winds. Their great pendulums swing and dangle, dancing to the leading flow. The pines, so straight and massive, stand in heights no human below them can see. They have stood the test of time. Rather than fight the winds, they have grown in a steadfast heart-iness, and have moved in rhythm. When the seasons lead them into the new, they do not fight against it, they adapt, becoming rugged and anchored. Once the trees are old enough and have grown deep roots, they are grounded and can overcome impressive storms. They adapt to what is around them, they accept the new and thrive within it.

When I begin to blow My winds of change over you, remember the stoic pines and their response to

45

change. Recall the strength and towering heights they have reached. You, too, should be moving, yet firmly rooted in Me. My children should be flexible to the many changes in life. They should not be so dependent on another that they lose their way when that person is gone. They should not be so complacent in their walk with Me that upheaval causes great stress. They should not be so ATTACHED to things and perceived safety nets that fear comes upon them, to the point of retreat, when these things disappear. No, My children should be so enfolded in Me for all these things, because I AM THEIR ALL. Then, when circumstances, people, and things change, they are able to pick up and begin afresh.

I have new things, great things, in store for each of My children, but how will you ever walk in them if you get knocked down with My winds of change, rather than flow with them? How will you ever know My mighty hand of provision and blessings awaiting you? How will you be molded into My image and earn the title of Triumphant Warrior? How will you ever truly know Me as your Refuge and Strength, your Ever-Present Help in times of trouble?

Augusta, Maine, Togus Pond—Afternoon Canoe

I call forth a sense of adventure in My people! For I am creative, not merely full of life. I AM LIFE! So why would I desire a lackluster life for My children? I call you to be eager and ready at any moment to launch out into new areas. Do not be trapped inland when there is a whole new life waiting for you to embrace. I am with you as you go out onto the waters.

Though finding your way to this camp has not been a smooth ride, My children, you have made it here, to this tiny speck of shoreline. That never seemed possible a few weeks ago back when the forest was so dense that you couldn't move without first swinging a blade before you. The path has been long, continuously uphill, and filled with debris, as it is the road less traveled. *But you have made it now, to the launching point.* Though the canoe is not the newest and could even use a few repairs, there is in your spirit the yearning to see My creation, My highest being worth it! Though your body may be uncertain of the ride, it is still worth the price. Though you have never been on these waters before, and don't know the course ahead, it is still worth the price.

Do you not enjoy the sun warming your body at the perfect temperature? How about the remote shoreline with only the trees dropping acorns for sound? How about My splash of green lily pads as your companions? *How about the release of pressure from the heated season in the valley?* My children, you would have never experienced this had you retreated and chosen the paved path which does not lead to this shoreline!

. Now is the time to ride along the waters. Allow Me to be your oars. I will guide your vessel into the areas through which only I can make a way. It is the only way for you, and this way is unbeknownst to any man, no matter how well-intentioned. This is a ride of faith and only I can guide you on it. Have complete reliance on Me, your Answer, your Breath, your Internal Drive; I have launched you forward into this place. I am the Father who will never fail to lead you in the most unexpected ways, to the most unexpected places. When I am your Oar, you will never have to worry about getting lost or being swept into the wrong direction. *My children I am ultimately leading you to My green pastures.*

6

More Rural Maine Messages

Washington, Maine—End of September

Fall is permeating the atmosphere. Previously, the touch of fall was a little here and a little there. Now it is steadily moving toward an overtaking of the area. *Life is taking on a different form through the death of the former season.*

Life also took on a greater degree through My death. It is the same with your life in Mine. The more you die to self and self's interests, the more life will embody you, powerfully touching others. So, through death comes new life, just as your physical death will bring a new life. Without Me, everything and everyone faces a death sentence. Here and now you will stay in a state of winter even though your body is still physically alive.

Truly those without Me are walking dead people. Not so with those in whom I dwell, *because I obliterated the concept of death!* The fall season now is not a desolate time, but a gift given to you to go inward and become new. The happenings of summer can leave you spinning in all directions, at times leading you away from Me. I beckon you now, come back to Me, letting all this fall from you.

Don't mourn the past or even look back. Understand, when all is removed from your life, then I can step first place into your life and dazzle you with My character. This happens when you are looking only to Me. What will you do when you are stripped of everything, like a tree in the fall? Will you panic and begin to search for available resources? Will you search for a person to fulfill your needs? From eternity's viewpoint, when everything has fallen from you, then you are in the least desperate state.

Remember, eternity's viewpoint is vastly different from the perspective of the temporal. It is during this time that My moving becomes heightened. As your idols are dropped, your focus is on Me, and you are dying to self. Be as a tree during this time, storing its energy during the winter. Plug into Me and you will burst forth with buds of continuous life after the death of self.

Vassalboro, Maine—Webber Pond Sunday Afternoon

I am showcasing sweet harmony to you on this peaceful afternoon. The rushing of summer's entanglements has ended, My children, and I eagerly move in for those who want to make their abode with Me. COME BY THE WATERS. SIT AND BE REFRESHED. I have adorned today, this very afternoon, in all its beauty; it is a call, a call for all who have ears. Come to My waters! I will bring a new song, a leaping of freedom, into the hearts of My people. No longer will they just talk about freedom or have an emotional experience. No, you will be engaged and participating with Me in My never-ending dance.

So, I speak to you now, COME ALIVE, DEAD BONES! Your scattered bones will begin to shake, the dust will be left behind. Ligaments, muscles, tissues, and skin will form, YES, from a dead man to one more full of life than a newborn babe! You will have no fear of stumbling, nor of performing incorrectly, because nothing will have your gaze but ME. *My lead dance oversteps any mistakes or obstacles. I create a new setting,* just as you are looking at today.

Today is a scene from My marvelous dancefloor. It is alive with beauty, brimming with life; joyful music is in the air. *My laughter is impressed upon the hearts of My people.* The water has a sparkle no man-made lake could rival. Our background is lit in bright blue, with white clouds moving to the beat. My birds are orchestrating the music, flying overhead, declaring My symphony. The swinging branches, grasses, and once-dead leaves all sway to the dance. Life is flowing all around you, unable to keep still, as My dancefloor explodes, leaving everything swaying. There is no longer a still, dead scene, but a scene that is engaged in LIFE, CREATIVE FLOW, TRULY *MY RIVERS OF LIVING WATER.* This is what happens when I lead the dance! In My people, there is always a current that will never stop flowing!

Appleton, Maine—Field of Christmas Trees

Pungent aroma of evergreen is in the air as young branches are pruned. Colors of hardwoods border the field of Christmas trees. Grasses and wildflowers succumb to fall's growing intensity. The sun finds an opening in the clouds, viewing the impressive scene. The scent lingers and the soft breeze disperses the traces, sharp and refreshing.

I am the Aroma of Life to all who stop to breathe Me in. I am a distinct and unique Aroma; as I permeate the seeker his burden is lifted, his step lighter.

I rejuvenate the weak, quietly giving strength as they stop, linger, and breathe in My life-giving scent. This is all you need do: Stop. Pause from the busyness of life, put your worries to the side, inhale My Breath of Life deeply into your lungs, and I will saturate your being. This is how I make My abode in you.

I don't stop at one area and forget the rest of you. No, no, no. Ha! I am Creator of you and I know every secret place hidden to man and even those unbeknownst to you! *How could I possibly overlook and neglect any detail of you, apple of My eye?*

I am not a God who gives a temporary feeling that washes away when the suffocating scent of despair moves in. No, My Breath of Life will flood your entire being, permanently, fixed, and **eternal**. You will bring forth a robust aroma as you brim over with My infilling, just as the pruned Christmas trees exude a resin that overtakes the air around them. Yes, your mind is brought from a scattered place to a grounded and secure foundation that is love, joy, and peace.

You will begin to outpour new health and vitality. Your heart will start a new beat, no longer simply pumping blood to the physical body, but *pumping My very aroma of eternal life into your soul.* This aroma is what enables you to dance through and out of tribulation, to proclaim My goodness when natural circumstances send you blow after relentless blow. My vision and plan for you is then in full display, as you manifest into conquering and warriors sold-out to My kingdom, warriors decorated in cloaks of mere humility in the natural eye, *but victoriously drenched in My aroma in the unseen realm!*

Searsport, Maine, Moose Point Park—Solace of the Sea

Today's beauty is unparalleled as one sets their gaze across My vast expanse of ocean waters. The sun creates the illusion of drifting diamonds, dazzling the viewer. The water is coming in with gentle waves. One can see a duck floating alone, but suddenly, he is gone, darting away and disappearing from view. A seagull perches on a patch of water-locked land. Red, yellow, and orange-hued leaves are spread across a canvass of evergreen branches.

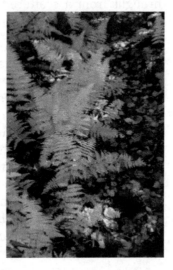

The color schemes and dimension of depth lay far beyond what the natural eye can see. It's a message from Me, Original Artist and Father of Creation. Ferns, once bright green, are now dancing across the forest floor in their yellow fall attire. There is a small, twisty trail of red leaves leading through the brigade of ferns and ending above a rocky coastline. Piles of seaweed cover rocks of all sizes and shapes. The setting is one of solace for what lies hidden amidst these woods. Pretty, maintained trails go several directions, each a pleasant experience.

Suddenly, *without warning,* the scene changes. The woods on each side of the trail have been demolished, their beauty gone. Butchered trees lay scattered, left in their own upheaval. Nobody has been back to straighten and make the woods beautiful again. As if in a hostile manner, large, splintered pieces of oaks stick up from their stumps. Someone has been here and left a massacre. This part of the trail is marred. Any form of life is barely thriving. The only thing noticeable here is death.

✝ *Keep walking, My Child, don't get off course or keep your focus on the death around you.* I know it comes as a shock in this otherwise beautiful place, but if you stop and gaze on this scene, you will become mesmerized; you will be taken in by the shock of death around you. You will fall prey to this disillusionment, and death will enter your mind and take you in. You must keep walking, Child. DO NOT become fixated on the death around you. Even though you do not know when this scene ends, I do, and I am forever with you on this devastating walk.

Now look up and let your heart leap, because you've made it; you have passed through the Valley of the Shadow of Death! Now you can begin to see the patches of green in the trail. Keep going, My Child! Don't look back, or you, too, shall become the fate of Lot's wife, a pillar of salt.

Keep focused on the shreds of green blades of life in the trail. That is Me, and I am guiding you. The green in the forest is returning, regaining life again. Now you are at the end of this trail and you have come to a mighty, white pine. So impressive is this pine that it has been marked with a sign of honor, revealing it is over 100 years old and 160 feet high. This tree is an amazing accomplishment. One hundred years of winters, My Child! This tree has stood the test of time and has become a rugged tree, with so great a root system that it is holding an entire section of forest in place. Just a few yards away is the end of land, a cliff over My ocean waters. Once small, the tree struggled to survive the harshest historical winters, but now it thrives. It has learned to strengthen itself on the summer's harvest. NOW, more effortlessly, it sustains itself during the barren season. In fact, it supports others who are coming through the Valley of the Shadow of Death.

Had the tree given in and succumbed to the winters and died, countless others would be dead from the lack of support its root system now provides. It has massive, invasive roots; this tree has a great capacity to store its own energy! *This is My vision of you. This is your mirror, your reflection, after going through the trail of death!*

Washington, Maine—The Transition

All of nature is in quiet waiting. The great oaks, still in their green uniforms, anticipate being cloaked with their coats of many colors. The surroundings are all changing and these oaks also must go along with the new season. They will enter this season shortly, for the signs are all about. Their new coats will be clear markers of inheritance and lineage.

Raise your downcast face, Child. Give hope entrance into your heart! Look around. The peak season of fall is nearly in sight. Yes, it is a change, but embrace it fully, for the change is about to dazzle eyes that have gone blind. Congested airways now breathe in My crisp, clean fall air. Ears dulled by the roar of chaos and disorder are soothed by the drifting call of the songbird.

The mind, the soul, did you think I would leave those out, the most important facets of your being? Like a magnet I cover you, flood you, with my rays of sunlight. Yes, I am dispersing, disbanding, dissolving, and making these places new! These wounds could never be removed, except by Me. The array of the world's answers is merely bandages to cover and hide the wounds, but My sunlight exposes, making the infection flee. My potent rays dry up the wound, revealing a velvet area without any trace of scar left behind. Truly, Child, I make these areas MORE beautiful than if there had never been a wound at all. These areas will be so tender and receptive to My touch.

It will be a delight for My heart as I engage more intimately with you than ever before possible. I transition your gushing wounds into marvelous areas of flowing love, areas brimming over to now flood the rest of you with complete wholeness. Yes, this is how I, the Master Surgeon, operate. You are beyond restored. Expect to be more whole than before the battle, Child! This is how I perform surgery on you: I do not cut, I only trim to repair the disconnection. Don't let fear overcome you as I operate to bring change. My operations have GUARANTEED outcomes. So be at peace. Enjoy the perfect temperature today, the full sunlight, and the beginning stages of color, as you head into My full-blown covering of the coat of many colors.

Maine, rural spot – The Invitation

The abandoned house stands in silence, but the scene leaps at the viewer like a deafening cry. No sounds can be heard, nevertheless, the message of a life once full of hopes is all about. There are raised beds with veggie plants and a bountiful harvest, but the beds are full of weeds. An unkempt grapevine still climbs its arbor, an artist's touch of a painting decorates the barn. Apples lay scattered underneath their trees. The windows in the home reveal remnants of once-used items. It is the scene of shattered dreams.

What lies beyond? The road itself is peppered with lackluster homes. Debris lays scattered in yards, deteriorating mobile homes are in abundance, the paved tar leads to dirt. There is one ray of light on this disheartening road.

It is totally unexpected. It lies only a short distance from the abandoned house. A small trail points the way down to the water's edge. It is sweet relief, a certain surprise on this road. Sunlight shines upon the water below. The shoreline is reclusive, and few camps can be seen. A section of land in the near distance meets the water's edge. Trees are colored decorations. Grasses to one side are swaying in the water. It is surely a silent reprieve for this weary stretch of road.

Come to My waters. They are so close in reach. My heart longs to rescue these lives along the Road of Shattered Dreams. These lives were once babies and young children. They became youths with plans and dreams, but the thief came in to rob and steal. The dreams, once alive and part of the very DNA of these people, are now trampled and nearly forgotten. The only remaining memory of these dreams is an ache in their souls. The roaring lion has devoured the very traces of hope. Yet I am here, ever pointing the way to My water's edge.

I call to you, the ones in the darkest trailers. I reach My hand out to you, the ones whose lives are littered with debris. I offer you My undying love, those who live unnoticed down the dusty, remote road. Come to Me! Be filled at My water's edge. You are no less appealing to Me than when you were a tiny, innocent babe. You are wanted by Me. I am here, waiting with the ring for your finger, and my finest robe for your shoulders.

I long to kill the fatted calf and celebrate your return. All I ask is for you to come! Walk down My path to the water. I am here waiting to meet you and I will take care of the rest. Just come! Be with Me. *Beloved, I am continually watching and waiting for you to appear.*

Vassalboro, Maine—China Lake

The misty morning gives way to My lull over the waters. The lake appears as glass to those who glance in its direction. *But to those of you who stop and look deeper, you experience My hovering.* The gentle ripples of water are moving, and it is I, looking, ever searching, to make My abode with those who have eyes to see. You will miss Me if you pass by without stopping.

The trees rim the vast shoreline and beyond in their finest colorful adornments, giving honor, glory, and splendor to My name. Rocks jutting up from the water provide a resting place for the birds. They are drawn to their Creator. They are aware of Me and stop their flight, quietly still, basking in My light on this drizzly morning.

My creation has My very heartbeat in it. That is what causes it to grow and renew itself. It is Me in it, My active hand. *This is all My gift, My passionate lure to draw you away and commune with Me by the water's edge.*

7

Cape Cod Long Weekend Retreat

Cape Cod, Massachusetts, Rock Harbor — Mountain Ash Tree

To My dear, desperate ones: Those with shattered souls, whose hearts live every second with the physical pain of radiating grief; to those desperately teetering on a wire, about to fall into the abyss; to the parents whose child lays in the cancer ward; to the single mother about to lose her home; to those whose minds are fragmented with mental illness; to the discarded spouse; to the sex-trafficked youth in dungeons; to the drug addicted ones living in places unfit for beasts; to the long-forgotten prisoners in darkness; to all the throw-aways of society *To ALL of you with invisible chains, My dear ones, this is My love letter to you.*

I am as the majestic mountain ash tree, hugging the corner of the estate house. My arms expand as these limbs, filling the windows with My reassuring green gaze. The tree gives honor to Me; it is a display of My character. The limbs reach in all directions; they are not contained and withdrawn. They wrap around the bedroom, embracing it. My arms also reach in all directions. I fervently long for all people and I readily make the first move to you, offering you the hollow of My safety and the banner of My love.

For I am the only One who sees into the deepest folds of the heart, the untold secrets, the vaulted pain. I see the consuming desire for healing of these places. I understand the addictions, the behaviors, the habits [those things in you that cause others to scatter and give up hope]. All these things are merely desperate attempts at self-preservation and thwarting the pain from becoming all-disabling. *I know the wounds of the heart never truly heal without Me.*

I know you are not capable of making these terrible, pained areas disappear as though they never existed. I know only I can do that for you. So, I reach My arms out to you. In different avenues and creative ways, I reach and I reach, longing to see you whole, freeing you of the vicious outcomes of the dark one; his goal is nothing short of chaining you, a bleeding, defeated prisoner on the floor.

Beloved, listen to Me: You don't need to try to get up on your own. This is not about *self-help,* but *acceptance of My help.* The world teaches that you must help yourself, but I give you different advice. You need only take My hand. Remember, My yoke is easy and My burden is light. If you act and desperately attempt to stand on your own, Child, you will never reach the heights of your true potential. You must lean on Me.

My dear one, trust in Me with all your heart and lean not unto your own understanding. In all your ways, acknowledge Me and I will direct your paths. **This is your key to unlocking the prison chains**. It has nothing to do with self-reliance and one's own strength. Your will alone is no match for the blows of the assailing enemy! But with Me, your bolted lock to the prison of pain always releases, because I bought that key with the price of My life! My own blood, My very life, was worth the price of your eternal freedom. I counted the cost and You, My beautiful one, were worth every drop of My blood, every excruciating agony, every rejection I faced on the cross.

You are rightfully Mine, bought with the highest price tag, *the telltale sign of true love, the willful laying down of one's own life.* Your active acceptance of My outstretched hand permanently seals the contract, declaring you are now My irreversible bloodline!

Cape Cod, Massachusetts, Nauset Beach

Going by the calendar, today is the middle of October. Going by the weather, it is just the beginning of September. The sun shines freely over the vast shoreline, without one cloud of interference against its warming rays. The sand is so soft, and its top so warm. It is irresistible to free one's feet that will soon be tucked away in heavy coverings for many months.

The never-ceasing waves come in again and again with a diverse sound, both fierce and strong, yet melodious to the onlooker. The ocean waters stretch as far as the eye can see, down the coastline and beyond the horizon. Birds are in flocks and formations expertly floating atop the waves before the whitecaps form into thunderous crashes. The salt air, invigorating and reviving, *coats an unseen layer over mind, body, and soul.*

The ocean, a force so compelling, appears to do just as it pleases. It can be so calming, but also so relentlessly unforgiving to anyone's slightest mistake or carelessness. The head of a seal pops up amidst the waves. His head shines in the sunlight. He is gone in an instant, then reappears elsewhere, just as suddenly, along the shore. His sleek body is well-adapted to the environment. His confidence is obvious as he precisely maneuvers the varying swells. He has no concern for the turbulence around him.

Learn this lesson from the seal, Child. Pay close attention to his amazing ability to thrive along these adverse waters. The waters, his environment, show him no mercy. He has no forecast; there is no warning given to him. He simply has learned to ride these waves, instead of being their victim. He is not pitifully flopping and being thrown in all directions. No, he is expertly calculated and adept in adverse conditions. *Rather than looking for an easy way out, he uses the turbulence to his advantage.* He has become a well-tuned vessel, and he impressively glides, using the crashing waves to move him **faster** along than he would go in peaceful waters.

My heart swells with a father's pride when I envision you living as this seal—effortlessly, confidently, displaying the ***power of fully accepting My love***. My love is the fuel and your acceptance is the lit match; when they come together, *you ignite,* and I course through your entire being, changing everything - perceptions, confidence, and character. Then you, too, become a fine-tuned weapon, burning through enormous and otherwise deadly pressure. These conditions would normally disable or kill a man, but when you accept My love without inhibitions, you become a conquering and highly honored soldier in My unseen kingdom.

Yes, as a result, rather than killing you, all these deadly forces pay tribute to you, as you overcome the traps devised and meant for death.

There is neither back and forth, nor double-mindedness anymore! This is when My children become cemented in surpassing degrees of honor and singlemindedness!

8

Rural Maine Speaks Again

Freedom, Maine—Blueberry Barrens in Autumn

No longer a blue field, this is stunning, brilliant red at its highest hue. Trees of many colors border and surround the ex-

pansive field, their arms extending, debuting the magnificence. The red spills over, touching all the once-green blueberry bushes, bathing them into a new creation. They are now even more beautiful, offering for the eyes to awaken and surpass their ability of mere physical sight. Eyes open to a new dimension as the incredible scene causes a reaction of delight. *Keen vision emerges.* It is a wonder how death can carry more beauty to these blueberry barrens than ever before.

My blood also releases new life. My physical death was wrought with so much red that it spilled over, touching the ground below Me as I carried the cross. My body was no longer the same color. My blood was covering it, the cross stained.

As I hung on the cross, death was no match for Me. My sacrificial death leads – and continues to lead – all to new life for those who choose it. When you come to the cross and accept Me, My blood covers you also. You are no longer the same; a light now emits from you, distinguishing you as it shines from your eyes!

New vision emerges as you begin to experience the reality of life with Me.

Nature takes on a new, alluring world. Colors heighten to otherwise unnoticed delights. Sounds become musical. Smells invigorate. Perception has changed to enlightenment. You are eager to walk in My creation as you are filled with awe of Me. Relish and divulge; bask in Me today. As you do, you shall radiate a fresh color at which the weary world will stop and behold in awe. The death of your former self will be no match for the intensity of color I shall display through you!

Benton, Maine

The strip of pink light glows against black-blue clouds. Birch trees line the horizon and create a mesmerizing canvas, their shadowy silhouettes motionless. It is a silent night. The previous rain and raw temperature have driven all forms of life to shelter and to wait. *My presence is here, even though you may not feel Me.*

67

There is no warmth in the air, but still I hover. The pink strip surrounding the horizon, the most prominent feature of the evening sky, is My love spilling down onto the earth, overseeing My beloved creation. I am the highlight of this evening, the Light of Life, no matter what the season may bring. I am the Everlasting One, the Illumination in the dark night.

Maine—Last Days of October

A shifting filters into the atmosphere, a penetrating cold rain that overtakes the area. The immediate bite invades the air. The cold seeps deep into the body, and the effects of it can only diminish *after entering a heated place*. The sensation goes into the core of the body, changing the chemistry.

The markings of this weather are obvious. The leaves' colors have dulled and many have fallen and blown away, leaving trees now unable to hide their form. Life has withdrawn. Insects have disappeared. Small animals have found shelter in unbeknownst places of darkness. Signs of larger animals are around. At times they show themselves, but they are also gearing up for the season ahead, storing the last bits of nutrition they can still find. The warmer days of their frolicking have ended. The accommodating rays of sunlight, once lasting into the deeper evening, have vanished. Darkness dominates.

At what time did this occur exactly? What specific moment did the fall commence its full reign?

Coldness can just as stealthily enter the heart of man. Many things can cause this to happen. A thread of jealousy turns into full-blown hatred. A disappointment manifests into a sorrow so consuming to the spirit of man that he takes his own life. A sadness becomes a disabling depression. Grief turns into a voracious bitterness that becomes the ruling perception. Anger fuels and flares into a murderous rage. A once sane person fragments and becomes deranged from circumstances. In this life, Child, a person will endure all ranges of highs and lows. The highs can be exhilarating, the lows devastating. Those who are not grounded in Me will be molded by these situations. They will become less like Me and My attributes. They will fall prey to varying degrees of these emotional states.

You must live under My wing. There is no other place you can be safe from self when the frigid cold explodes upon you. Reach for this truth, Child, as if you are drowning and grasping the life-saving float. Understand, if you allow your emotions to reign, they will kill you.

Emotions are never to be trusted because they are based in self, and self is an empty pit never to be satisfied. Self always seeks its own pampering. It is never able to look beyond its own immediate gratification, *no matter what price.* Self is totally blinded to truth. The price can be death to another person or the destruction of anything in its way. It does not matter, as long as self is fed.

If you are not walking in Me, then you risk being self's next victim. Self will justify its actions and behaviors relentlessly, always in defense of them. Self will call wrong what is right, and call right what is wrong. Self will feel entitled to all lusts. Self will list reasons why negative emotions are acceptable, and then feast on these emotions until they become the frigid hand of death to all who come near them.

69

But My Child, fear not, because those who are grounded in Me, and not their own emotions, will transform into strength, honor, and dignity. Their faces will shine from My indwelling; no shame or defending of their own character will be found in them. When the sorrows of life strike, they will float upon My wings *and the poison meant for death, shall drip to the ground*!

This is the moment in which peace that passes all understanding becomes much more than a poetic phrase, **it becomes your identity**. Willfully choosing the higher path and surrendering even your desires for justification of your emotions, for these things are left outside as you gain access under the safety of My wing. So, My dear One, choose this day whom you will serve.

I have now shown you plainly what hangs in the balance. Self is the pathway leading to eternal death. Surrendering is the path I took. It is the only pathway leading to transformation in this life, and My eternal magnificence of pure satisfaction. The warmth of love you shall emanate from under My wing will melt even the most arctic of seasons in your life!

Augusta, Maine, Arboretum

The afternoon stretches and beckons the end of day. The sun's rays showcase once during this hike, yielding a dose of warmth. The grey clouds eventually gain victory. Rain appears imminent. The path shows signs of fall's height of glory, now over, the peak of its beauty now revealing what lies in store. Leaves are thicker on the ground than in the trees. The few leaves still attached have turned yellow, orange, and bronze. A small entrance on the path leads to a huge, green field where, upon entering, you will feel the wind, hear the birds, and behold the still-green grass across the expanse.

Come onto My path, Child. Choose to leave the former trail behind you. That past is only wrought with death now. Just as the beauty of fall was a spectacular show, such was the past; it was a show that ended. Come onto My trail that will never end in death. My path leads away from death and into new life! If you live in the past and choose not to go forward with Me, you will also become as dead as the things on that path. My path leads away from death and into marvelous light. ✓

Yes, the birds still flitter and sing. The breeze has heightened, bringing new life into the body. The tamaracks have shed most of their green, but little pinecones are still alive on the branches. *You cannot tell in which direction My path curves ahead. It does so in unforeseen places. Keep following My path Child, because no matter where you've been, I will always bring you to the foot of the cross.*

At the edge of the field you can see a wooden cross. *The "cross" may have been placed as a trail marker by man, but I had it placed here as a reminder to the souls who travel this path.* Yes, keep your face on the cross, the prize, and at the end of your walk on earth, you shall inherit nothing less than the adoration, zeal, passion, and expanding love of Heaven, ME! Indeed, you shall experience all these attributes and the far-reaching ones of which earth has no knowledge.

Hallowell, Maine, Vaughn Woods

The woods are thick with the smell of fall leaves. The earthy, calming scent brings clarity of mind. A maple tree has deposited a patch of bright yellow leaves on the trail, and they lay amidst the fallen golden-brown ones. The trail twists on. It is a sunny day and the crisp fall air is now fully-engaged. The water can be sensed before seeing it; the air cools and dampens. The smell of the water's flowing movement heightens, and can now be seen spindling down its various falls. The gushing of tumbling water and its liberty of movement dominate the whole section of woods. The noise is rushing, the smell invigorating, the flow is infusing all who walk by with a fresh partaking of life. It leaves nothing untouched.

The flow of life in Me also gushes and spills forth to all who walk nearby. I leave nothing untouched. After experiencing Me, you are indeed a new creation! Truly, the things of the world grow dim and I take first place in your all-consuming mission of more. More, Child? Oh, I have so much more that the vocabulary on earth cannot describe My more! Child, there are yet to be words to explain My attributes, because they exceed all of earth's concepts and knowledge.

My love reaches further than earth could possibly conceive. I make all things new. When you are drawing from My flow as your first source, My hydration will bring life to all parts of you. Your problems seem insignificant, as My peace that passes all understanding floods the debris, repelling your condition of disillusionment. Even the pleasures of this world, to which you are so drawn, will become blurry and less appealing, as My flow flings these lures away from you; My flow reveals a much more desirable, insurmountable, constant joy. My flow is unlike the earthly pleasures that bring a temporary state of happiness.

Once in My flow, your perception changes to that of deeper and deeper reality and truth. Because of this, *you* change. It is a natural occurrence, neither forced, nor demanded. The burden is lifted as your nearsighted vision becomes clear. Your eyes will change from the clouded, blurry blindness, to sight exceeding an eagle's shocking clarity of perception and depth. Yes, Child, you will go beyond vision, such as the capability of an x-ray, seeing what lies in and beyond the circumstances presented to you. This is why peace and joy flood your being so effortlessly; My waters sweep the fears out and replace them with the reality of Who I am. You, in Me, dominate any circumstance, temptation, and emotion. My waterfall eradicates all these things in Your path!

9

Month of Messages in Southport Island

Southport Island, Maine

Who causes the waters to stir across the shoreline, into the deep and beyond the abilities of human vision? Who gives the seagull the urge to cry out, with the resounding chime echoing across the picturesque lull? Who released the sun to rise and heat this cove with its warm embrace? How have these evergreens-maintained tenacities enough to remain standing, surpassing the rocky terrain and salty conditions? Who pushed back the waters out to sea, laying bare the gritty sand shining in the light?

Each bush, each blade of green life, each stone upon the shore, and the breeze awakening the quiet cove are all by My hand. I am an active God in My creation. I never walked away from it, as some assume. It is a living, breathing extension of Me! It is all for you, My people, My masterpieces.

Far more intricate than the vast coast are My people. I made you a physical, spiritual, mentally-heightened, and emotional creation. You have the greatest capacity for love of all my creation. You have the ability to fashion My master design within your life.

I am always, forever, permanently, with you. I actively guide you all the way, just as My hand creates every stroke of nature's touch upon your day. I am moving ahead of you, paving the way with My outstretched arms; I am ignited and fueled by My all-consuming passion for you. My spirit hovers over the ocean waters, further than you can see, Child, and covers the earth. So, I am actively with you and ahead of you into the future, beyond what you could ever imagine. I am with you outside all limits, even that of physical death on earth. I am so much greater. My heartbeat is aligned with yours. Your being is always enmeshed with Mine. I never leave you! My nest for you need never empty.⌒

Southport Island, Maine—Small Beach Cove

The November daylight dissipates and dissolves from the Maine coast. The early evening has brought on the invading darkness, easily overtaking the area of thick evergreens. The trail leading to the water's edge follows no set rules; it turns and bends and rises where the traveler knows not. The ground on either side is covered with a story-book, fairytale-like moss, imparting the message that anything may lay in wait. It is a heavy and thick carpet that depresses inches when walked upon. The darkness nearly swallows anyone walking on the trail.

But then, in the distance, in the areas between the long trunks of thick trees and fantasies of the mind, the scene begins to change. Oh my, what delight of the soul, an igniting of the spirit is felt amidst the darkness.

Ha Ha! Yes! It is I, **invading the scene**. A dazzling, bright orange-pink suddenly splashes onto the background of the woods. A new life invades those who choose to walk through this darkest of trails. It is a most uncertain trail. Human eyes are unable to decipher what lies hidden in the dark crevices and the covering of trees. A black mass of water stands on part of the trail, holding prisoner the decaying stumps. But the desire for the shoreline overrides it all.

This desire is to see the magnificent beauty of day, succumb to the evening cast. *Yes, this is the Way, and the color, for which no replica exists, through the trees is the Light of Me!*

Have I not promised to walk with you through the valley of the shadow of death? Did you expect Me to leave you for the night to consume you? No, I walk you through these trails in life and lead you to the most unexpected and unparalled destinations. I awe you with My marvelous surprises.

The glow of light becomes stronger and more powerful than the darkness, as the trees recede behind and the trail opens to the beach cove. Brilliant color appears across the expansive horizon, highlighting the islands in the distance. The color knows no bounds; it is no match for any darkness. This is the way indeed, My Child.

The walk here is never easy, but it is undeniably worth the darkest and harshest conditions to reach this incredible viewing. *The scene is so powerful, it goes past merely visual and becomes manifest as it rushes into the airways of the viewer.* As a dry twig sparks a fire, so the scene ignites with Me! The fire engulfs everything in sight, just as My light is cast across the ocean waters and into the darkness on this November evening. I am the highest form of illumination that floods the darkest of nights, re-creating every situation and every person. They shall come from darkness and leave glowing and infused! My saturation will emerge and trickle from them. They shall go back onto their once-darkened trails and shine the way for others to find My shoreline, *the doorway to My transforming horizon of color.*

Southport Island, Maine, Small Harbor Cove - Creative Flow

A stirring, a great stirring, sends the ocean waters rushing in all directions. Far from shore, the powerful white explosions launch upwards, as the great waves collide with the rocks. Thunderous dimensions of sound overtake the environment; everything is charged. The wind gives its resounding flare as it darts through every crevice and twig. The flow rushes past the cove and continues its momentum, gliding and finding bare spaces between the trees before continuing onward in its reign. The massive trees dance in a newfound freedom as the wind ignites its creative flow over all the area. Nothing is left untouched.

The birds sing out in approval, delighting in the reviving sweep. Swirling and dancing leaves spiral into the flow. A creature darts up and around and through its terrain, then freezes, motionless, its complete attention on the message in the air.

This is the outcome when My hand begins to stir the waters. This is what happens when I reach out and begin My stirring! Slowly, and calculated I touched the waters this morning and they responded to My motion. My beautiful expanse of ocean waters, how they resemble Me and My mighty inflowing of passion! Did you know My own nature was wrought into these ocean waters when I surveyed the mass of nothingness, and poured out My very Spirit into the deep?

Yes, these ocean waters are the outlet for My love. Mighty and rushing, so full of zeal at times. Other times My gentle touch is felt along the quiet bay. Both demonstrate a powerful experience, yet in very different ways. My love is poured out to you in these different ways along the seasons of your life. My creative flow is unseen, yet it douses the area as an invisible liquid. All of nature senses and responds to My stirring upon the waters. Nature reaches out in a ravishing hunger to devour My creative flow and be rid of the curse of Eden. Will you also come into the flow and respond to My stirring?

Today, I send out My creative call to you. It is for all those who desire to flow in the highest form of frequency, defying the mundane barriers and limitations to which you have remained so accustomed and chained. You want more? *My more surpasses beyond so much more than this lifetime can only contain as a mere threshold of the flow I impart!*

Barter Island, Maine, Porter Preserve—My Playground

This is the playground I have created. Yes, you heard Me right. Did you think I was above fun and shrieks of delight and laughter? I created laughter, delight, and fun. I created those wonderful emotions and highs of the heart. These things are My avenues for the health of your whole being. Research by man is just catching on to the gravity of the effects these things have on a person. The research may be new, but the truth is as old as the creation of man.

Did you think I would want you to live in somber chains of piety? Did you think I would want you to spend your waking moments in a lifeless church, in what resembles a funeral service, and in which you were only able to remain awake because of the hard, miserably uncomfortable pew underneath you? Truly, anyone with this conception of Me doesn't know Me!

I created Eden. I created My people to be enmeshed in a paradise brimming with life! Beautiful and vibrant food was all around, decorated in a lush setting. My finest artistry was the abode for My people. They did not live in squalor. They did not live in isolation. They did not toil in relentless conditions. Every day, they lived in awe of the vibrant life around them. Their communication far exceeded any of the interactions after their fall. They had perfect understanding and an infilling of joy that permanently filled their hearts *they had direct communication with ME.*

This place you visit today, a tiny speck on earth, a shoreline on an island in Maine, is a place for My children, both young and old, to unwind and explore all the hidden crevices, coves, twists, and turns.

Maneuvering through the changing landscape and coming to the ends of all these paths, I bring you a variety of breathtaking views. My crowning touch upon this paradise is the aroma of salty air filtering through evergreens, intermingled with fall leaves.

The trees have grown in different directions, due to diverting their roots from great rocks and tough soil beneath. Their branches can be used as seats or handles to propel oneself along. The different channels and bays are a lure causing one to view the curiosities deposited from the ocean's depths. The terrain goes from mossy and soft to jagged and solid.

The eyes are delighted and alert as each new bend boasts various plant life. My woods are so thick here that the trails are delightful and fantasy-like, *expanding the minds of My children into new dimensions of My ever-lurking possibilities.* The trails maintain unseen curves, where robust roots spread across areas of packed earth and large rocks. The green, nearly touching one's shoulders, shoots up in great heights.

Enjoy your experience here; allow your mind and soul to expand and leap for joy in My playground. I say unto you today, *Come out of the shackles of religion, society's belief systems, and the steel doors that have closed your mind.*

Come into MY world! Allow Me to strip away those things that hold you hostage. Come in and enjoy My world of laughter, love, and My never-ending reign of life in its fullest form!

Ocean Point, Maine

The elements of nature collide and impart a surge to the senses. Sight, sound, feeling, and smell are instantly awakened to new levels. The sun sends its rays over the ocean setting below. The waves make contact with the rocks along the stretch of earth where land meets water. The crashing sound covers any other noise. The water sprays up to refresh anyone nearby. The salty air goes deeply into every living thing. The winding road ahead now belongs to a ghost town. The past is here, and the new season has made most human life scatter and settle somewhere else, a place where summer will never forsake them.

Massive trees sway in the wind. Green grass can still be seen on this spring-like day. The rocky shoreline goes on and on. A surprise message is painted upon a property: "Not all those who wander are lost." The poignant message is in its rightful place on earth; it defies the status quo of life and dares anyone to go down a new, unfamiliar path. Such is the unspoken theme of Maine.

Rose bushes have mostly yellowed. The roses have long been rosehips, and now this stage finds them shriveling to nothing. The bushes can be seen all over the area, dotted with the little red balls. Then, amidst some of these bushes, a surprise is waiting. All by itself, one little rose has managed to flower. It is alone, all fellow company is past, and few admirers are even there to walk by and notice. But the flower remains, in plain sight, pink and open under the sunlight. Some green leaves can still be seen on it. The delicate beauty is impressive in a location where all other flowers, and even heartier plants have passed.

Today, many are not willing to go through adverse conditions and seek My higher paths. They would rather indulge their flesh, not realizing that in doing so, they are forgoing My very best for them. Not only

My best on earth for them, but most importantly, My eternal best.

Only I have the real view of eternity. This is why you should trust My voice over all others, including your own. Leave human reasoning aside; I am far beyond that. My reasoning is more expansive than the ocean waters themselves. I know how emotions and flesh can cause you to quickly lose your vision, and ultimately relinquish your highest path on earth. *If I am not in the forefront of your decisions, then take My warning: This will happen. It is impossible for you to take the highest path without learning from Me which direction to go each day.*

You can be sure there is no other way of finding this path. No matter how seasoned another person may be in their walk with Me, how wise it seems to the world, or even how good and moral it appears, the way is *not* as obvious as one may assume without My hand pointing you. Remember there is a way that seems right to man, but in the end, it leads to death.

This is most certainly true of man's good and humanistic deeds. Your good deeds are as filthy rags in My sight. I say this because I am so holy and My intentions are so pure. In the human fallen condition, it is not possible to perform any deed with a totally pure heart, aside from being in relationship with Me. Do not be discouraged by this; I love you nonetheless. Instead, be *encouraged* in knowing that when you find My voice you have found The Way.

My way may seem incredulous and even ridiculous to man, but on the day of accounting, those who have chosen to follow My voice and heed My direction will never regret this decision. When you see Me for Who I am, the only thing that will matter to you, instantly and forevermore, will be passionately following Me. I am pure Love that covers all desires, all wants, all needs, and every facet of man.

I created your facets. I am the only One to fill your places to overflowing. All else is counterfeit. You will know it is counterfeit when your initial delight fades, your soul hungers, and you begin your search for fulfillment all over again. I am the Living Embodiment of pure satisfaction that never dulls.

Southport Island, Maine—King Tide

A heightened anticipation surges through the fallen world as I shine the intensity of My great moon nearer to earth, exposing in the night what would normally be hidden. The waters respond to my gravitational pull and they part, engulfing greater portions of mass on the shorelines. Areas that normally remain dry are submerged.

A fresh indwelling will be deposited upon the shorelines, disclosing driftwood, human remnants, even new treasures that were hidden gifts in the deep of the darkest waters.

Now I have commanded those deep places to release! I call these hidden gifts forth to reveal themselves. As one walks on my shoreline after weathering these conditions, I will bring My manifest dreams into the physical hands of My people! Yes, after this great king tide, there remain beautiful and unique remnants of My touch upon the land. The very traces

of Me are the shining wonders along the shoreline and beneath the sprawled seaweed.

At first sight after the recesses of the tide, one can easily make the mistake of seeing only scattered debris. But I tell you, do not just glance. *Gaze* into the new surroundings. *If you do not see the result as I see the result, you will leave disillusioned, but* allow Me to shine My perception through your gaze. You will see amidst the washed-up logs, yellowed bushes, and sticks, a color brighter than any color in the peak of the summer. See a shining ball so brightly colored candy-red that a maraschino cherry comes to mind. It is a rose hip, one of the most beautiful and fragrant flowers along the summertime coastal shores.

During the fall season, it turns into a bright orange ball to celebrate. Then it begins its descent and shrivels. This rosehip today is the last one. It has survived all the seasons, still clinging to its browned stem amidst the lackluster debris. This rosehip, which would normally be a memory now, has survived, having been immersed in Maine's November king tide. It wears its color as a symbol of honor, its tiny essence shining among the surrounding dull colors.

I, too, cause waters to rise as a king tide. These waters are not meant to destroy, but to infill My believers with newfound heights of courage, stamina, and honor. After I pour Myself out and flood the environment, you also are left more brilliant than ever possible through any human endeavor. *My liquid peace will leave you so saturated that no element on earth, or beyond, will have the intensity to evaporate it, even from the hairs on your head.*

Southport Island, Maine, Beach Cove— The Gift

The November morning heralds unusual warmth on the coast of Maine. The walk down the thick trail is delightfully energizing, as if one might feel the cool of the evergreens awakening from their damp slumber. The birds are on their various perches singing as heartily as though introducing spring. The rays of sun can now be seen as the trail gives way to the shining horizon. The waters are steadily losing their dark, ominous, nighttime color as the sun melts the overcast from foreboding to sparkling. The sandy

87

shoreline touches the glass-like water, revealing all that has lain hidden in the night.

In the treetops, crows make their sounds, echoing their raspy calls over the cove; seagulls on their tiny islands out to sea reply a greeting. This moment, this morning, is My most intimate love-gift, My very Self being poured out and joined with you.

Boothbay, Maine, Ovens Cove Trail

There was a desire in your soul today, as in the hearts of some of My children, to experience My All. A lingering question is the driving force for today's hike: *"What if there is unexpected beauty to be held in this place and I were to miss out?"* So, for this reason, My Child, the very longing in your soul is what has brought you here today. It is love for Me when you go out of your way to be with Me, even when you don't know what the trail may bring. You go along the trail and are energized by your quest for the very best of Me. You wish never to relinquish Me, the ultimate prize, for security and comforts. No, there is a truth which radiates in your soul, although the light can become dull from bitter disappointment and life's outcomes.

Still that light never goes out; it's a desire for more, more, and more of Me. It is a desire that is an empty pit, aside from My indwelling. Regardless of when life is wonderful, mundane, or even filled with grief, this light remains your driving force propelling you to Me. Today, I display to you My marvelous surprises on this trail, mimicking the path in life.

Chosen today is the harder of the trails, the path along the edge of land. The inland path is wider and boasts easier walking. There is no view of the water along the way. Yes, one would see the water eventually, but why not take the harder path, in light of drinking in every view, every experience along the way? *Why not take My highest route, the one that gives the actual experience of Me? It is more than just a shortcut, which actually cuts you off from Me.*

In the initial views, the tidal waters are stagnant. Many would not even care to see them at all. The trail is covered with slippery, paper-like fall leaves. Roots and rocks protrude in all directions. The path is steep and winding. It is mandatory to hold on to some trees along the way, *just like it is to take My hand along this path.*

The trail leads to the very edges along the way. The drop-offs are dizzying. The imagined tumble makes one shudder. The water is not impressive at this stage, it is an inlet channel, filled with muddy-looking water and rocky portions along the way down. This goes on until an attractive footbridge comes in view through the trees. It is recognizable from the map, *just as My map, the Bible, will impart illumination to you in life.*

The sight of the bridge is a welcome one, and the water has now changed. It is moving, and the flow has caused clarity inside it. The bridge is now within the next few steps. Yes, it was worth it. The view is beautiful and better than imagined. Coming to this place today brings immediate gladness. There is full sun and shining water. Enjoy a resting spot on the bridge as you take in and experience the view.

I will bring you times of reprieve of the soul, even in the harshest battles of life! Shortly after crossing over the bridge, the prime view comes in sight and it is an intersection of tidal river waters. Immediately upon seeing this, the scene appears serene and quiet. The motionless trees are all around and the sun lends its comforting warmth on this November day.

There is no wind today. The water is smooth and could pass for ice, but then a small driftwood is spotted. It is moving and moving fast! The water appears calm, but it is just the opposite. The current is rushing. At the point of different intersections along the way it swirls powerfully.

Life can seem stagnant at times, like murky waters. Life can seem brutally mundane at times. Do not lose your gaze; keep your eyes fixed, and you will surely see the swirling of life, indicating I am indeed here. I am present and proactively moving your life. Do not be deceived and lose heart from the lack of movement in your present experience. Understand I am moving the waters. I am making a way out of the dark, murky, stagnant waters and into the great deep. Ha, yes, I am moving and touching in such a profound way that you could become frightened by My massive flow. But know I will propel you into new areas and new realms that you never knew existed. My path is unforeseen, unknown to man, but keep your gaze! Keep following the path as I create this current that cannot be stopped and can only move you in one direction, and that is forward.

The walk continues back over the bridge into new territory. The magnificent view of the water's flow continues until the trail goes back around and away from this mighty flow. It is amazing; the same body of water becomes more and more narrow. Now it becomes even smaller, to the point of a tiny stream with little rocks at the bottom. The stream flows peacefully

Figure 1. *An Owl Sporting amongst Leafless Shrubs*

with the bottom clearly visible, even from a distance.

There is a desire to put one's feet into the pleasant waters and enjoy the surrounding peace. The trail leads away from the water going up, with a final ascent onto rougher terrain. The woods are now thick and the feeling of wilderness floods in quickly.

*You will go through seasons of wilderness, but the indwelling of My flow will become richly alive in you. Though you may not see it, nonetheless, it is in you, giving you the ability, arming your body with the stamina to put one foot after another. Continue on, **refusing to even acknowledge** there is any other way but Mine. I will surely lead you out of the wilderness and onto new ground.*

This is what the Lord says, He who made a way through the sea, a path through the mighty waters, who drew out the chariots and horses, the army and reinforcements together. Then they lay there, never to rise again, extinguished, snuffed out like a wick: "Forget the former things; do not dwell on the past. See, I am doing a new thing! Now it springs up; do you not perceive it? I am making a way in the wilderness and streams in the wasteland. The wild animals honor me, the jackals and the owls, because I provide water in the wilderness, and streams in the wasteland, to give drink to my people, my chosen, the people I formed for myself that they may proclaim my praise. (Isaiah 43:16-21)

Southport Island, Maine—Darkening Hours

Different seasons, the intensity of night, a damp chill in the air, and a host of other things in your environment can cause fear to enter your heart, fear of what is to come, and fear of what lies hidden in dark shadows. The carnal man is aware of the things in the natural realm that are able to devour him. He listens to the onslaught of fear-driven information from a variety of reputed sources. These sources have agendas and motives. Their hearts are not pure, no matter how infamous the name may be. The drive behind this fear-driven spew is often mammon, greed, ambition.

How I hate to see people ruled by the plot of mammon, and living their lives by one question, "What if?" People go to great lengths because of this question. They use their money to buy a future more protected and more ensured of success and safety. If only people realized these things are such a distraction in the realm of what lies in the real world. Truly, it is the things hidden in the unseen realm that have the power to bring down the stamina of the soul, thus gaining victory in both the seen and unseen.

The evening shadows tonight cast their power over the mind, tempting it down their trail. This trail is wild and always leads away from Mine. The creatures and spiritual powers of wickedness lie here on this trail, deceiving all who choose to walk this path. My path will lead you to truth and peace. The reality of who you are in Me guards you like armor from these treacheries. The things in the natural world that cause you fear, even the worst circumstances, are nothing compared to the dangers that lie in the unseen realm. So, I give you this warning today: Do not worry yourself over these things in this life; they have only the power of illusion.

Child, be far more concerned with the things that lie in wait for your very soul. If My people really knew this, they would turn off their entertainment screens, forgo their fleshly comforts, and stop pursuing perceived safety nets and man's rational planning. They would pursue Me with all their hearts, souls, and minds. They would go down My highest pathway for them, relishing My unseen gifts and pleasures. They would become enraptured in My love, as their spirits became **enlightened** to the reality and awe of life within Me.

The ones who have all the comforts and pleasures of this world are the ones who are really the poorest. So free yourself today from becoming this world's slave. The price of slavery to this world, and all its enchanting lures, is the highest price in the unseen realm. You see, My Child, the price of living for this world is the exchange of your very soul. Those who are living for the things of this world appear carefree and full of happiness, but in the unseen realm their souls are in chains. The chains also are bound to horrifying creatures along their chosen pathway, the pathway called "Fulfillment for the Here and Now."

This trail deceitfully fulfills only the flesh, as the denied soul cries out in anguish.

I give you this vivid picture today in My great love; I ask you, as Lover of your Soul, to loosen yourselves from all these entanglements. Be willing to give it all up. In so doing, you will gain true freedom, not the counterfeit "freedom" that so pervades this world. Come down My pathway, where your soul and heart will be ushered into relationship and everlasting pleasure in Me.

10

West Gardiner Speaks and Southport Island Continues

West Gardiner, Maine—Walk in Woods

I interrupt the walk today, highlighting My presence as I glide along the wind. My momentum infuses life into the great hemlock tree and every branch sways to the freedom. All of nature flows in worship of Me, sending a call out to those for whom I most yearn with a ravishing desire, My people. It is I, once again, making Myself tangibly known. Many have only knowledge of Me, losing out on life with Me. They know Me as a distant God, one who cannot be reached except in a metaphysical way, but not a day goes by that I do not extend My personal invitation. I watch the debut of your eyes opening each morning, and I see every other blink. I am with you until your eyes close a final time each night. I allow each breath to come into your lungs and allow the release as you exhale.

The redemptive power of Calvary surpasses all boundaries of time. My passion on the cross was evident for all to see. Today, and every moment since, My desire is no less dampened than at the time of My ultimate display of true love, as I laid down My own life. I have created all of nature as a call to bring you to Myself and experience an inflow that you shall never experience in any other highs of life. I am the ultimate filling of living water that leaves no crevice empty in you. I am the gushing river of true life, leaving all else, even what was once most consuming, now pushed and abandoned onto the riverbanks. As I overtake you and bring you to the reality of life living with Me, I fling away from you every extraordinary thing, every brutal disappointment, truly all pleasures and problems.

West Gardiner, Maine—Morning After Snowfall

You wake up to the display of My likeness today. The season is past color and many have already grown weary of the monotonous brown shades seen everywhere, on trees, roads, and fields. It is time. I gave the release for My likeness to come down as a blanket of respite for My travelers. Those traversing My paths will become aware of My touch this morning. I covered all the barren places with My brilliant, white coating of sweet reprieve. The snowflakes from yesterday have gathered and built up to present a new world to you. Yes, I always bring new life to the scene!

Today, I say to you, just as you experience the moments of feeling awe encased in My touch, also experience the joy that comes with today. Allow the white to cleanse dormant dreams, shifting them from a distant mirage in the mind to a reality before your very physical eyes. Enmesh yourself in Me today. Become so fresh that you, too, change the entire scene from dismal and mundane, to a life of rhapsody under My covering. Doing so will enable you to pass through whatever may come. You can even be mere inches away from death, but remain more than conquering, more than passionate, more than alive, as you shine and become My very likeness! You change the scene from dull to dazzling.

Southport Island, Maine - The Bright Morning Star

I am to you as the salt is to the coast. I encompass everything about you and in you. No part of your existence is without Me! I am all-consuming of every area: The light, the wholesome, the goodness, and the times of suffocating darkness. Last night's storm is over, My Child. *I display Myself with a regal entrance, as majestic as ever, the Bright and Morning Star, such that the storm of last night is immediately obliterated.*

The great fir trees, so thick in number, become blackened against the horizon of white and blue sky. They are no match for My light. I ascend through them, a brilliant orange, showcasing My divinity. My unseen presence is pouring through this place, more heavily than last night's rain. And I, the Great Ancient of Days, the Everlasting I Am, embrace this downtrodden area as lovingly as a mother holding her babe for the first time.

Known as the wind to man, I rush in, squelching the power of the storm. The cold, wet atmosphere, remnants of the storm's grip, have no power over Me. I effortlessly race through with My invitation; every human and all My beautiful creation is offered this prize. It is the prize with which the unseen realm is in a constant, furious battle, unlike the visible realm, where the battle is toyed with, rather than fought.

Whoever wants to live life in the fullest, I beckon you to immerse into My water. Dip your whole being into My great, salty waters, and you will *truly* become the new creation. Any counterfeits will not be possible when you *totally immerse*. The old ways will be as dung on your shoes. The things that once brought you great satisfaction will dim, as the truth of the pleasures of Me become your reality. Your stress and worries will be distant, as well, My Child, when you see I am bigger than the ocean itself. I expand further, with no end.

I have no shoreline. It is only an illusion that one can remain on the shoreline. If you are truly in Me, you are engulfed, over your head, as your eyes now see with perfect vision. I am the Ultimate Prize, the Bright Morning Star, *whose waters effortlessly saturate the impenetrable.*

West Gardiner, Maine—Snowfall Evening

White splashes onto the earth below. All is hidden under the cloak of nighttime blackness, except the bright white snowflakes. The once-darkened picture outside begins to illuminate. The heavy cast of darkness steadily retreats like a morning fog sensing the sun's heightening rays. All is silent, not a movement is heard, as the snow builds, flake upon flake. The new scene emerges. The darkened, ominous, great evergreens stand in their new attire, no longer foreboding or seemingly hiding a sinister presence. Their new transformation boasts an illuminated height, now towering in an endearing protective stance over the habitat below. *The environment is no longer a darkened January night, it is now a message of warmth, bold in its unseen power over the coldest of nights.*

No matter how dark the night, cold the temperature, difficult the terrain, or powerful the environment, it is no more difficult for Me stepping into the scene. In fact, I only enlighten more brilliantly when the darkness is blackest. I appear to shine even greater in a blackened valley. My brightness becomes noticeable, even to the blind. *I overtake the scene, which goes beyond mere change. You see, it becomes My very likeness!* Do not let the blackness seep into your mind, eroding all hope from your soul. I am here, and with Me there is always hope. I am Faithful and True. I am the Creator of Hope.

My presence comes down with each snowflake. The intensity gains until the scene becomes the fresh, new reality! I am the Reality of Life. *For those who wait on Me, I will gain in intensity and no scene will be able to escape My infilling. I AM the ultimate Game Changer, the Master of the Game of Life! I have plans and destinies for all My players and they shall come running, like lost and famished lambs, into a field of green, when their blindness collides with My dazzling, irresistible presence.* ✓

Southport Island, Maine

The heat of the sun comes as a pleasant shock on this day, ushering visions of fantasies nearly into reality. The air is clean and the powerful waves can be heard crashing through unseen trails. Snow is a scarcity here. It is obvious the winter has not yet claimed control over this area. The walk down the trail to the cove is a delight, as the body has come from another location, one bound in winter's steel grip on this very same day. The trail advances and so does the wind. It gushes forth and culminates into a full-blown display of power as the trail ends. The waves are impressive;

the chops come pounding in. Sprays of white can be seen on the shore and distant rocks.

You do not know the origin of these waves, just as you cannot possibly foresee what lies ahead in your life, but I do. I watched the *exact miniscule motion* begin the stirring of every wave you see, and those you do not see. I know the exact beginning of every alteration of your journey. You may be able to make some wise choices, but they are in no way comparable to My Holy Spirit leading your life! Truly, you are far better off with eyes that cannot see and ears that cannot hear, yet following My lead. Perfect hearing and 20/20 vision are no comparison to My Holy Spirit. How can the revelation of truth and My guidance be on the same scale as man's mortal senses?

My Holy Spirit knows all, from beginning to end. What could possibly hold more value? My Holy Spirit is all wisdom, incapable of mistakes. Again, I say, what comparison has man to offer against such? My Holy Spirit is passionately in love with your well-being, unconditionally sold out to your soul. Where can you find this all-consuming, ever-present, constant love *truly* in the heart of any man? What I offer is far beyond any type of human emotion or love. The most tender and protective mother cannot even touch the hem of My cloak of love that covers you with a completely selfless devotion. I am more precious than silver, more costly than gold, more beautiful than diamonds!

Child, the light of one lone star in a black canvas of sky is more revealing onto the earth than the human vocabulary is of Me. Communication with Me is more intimate than any words you ever exchanged. My direction does not require words, as human leading does. My direction begins with a stirring in your deepest, innermost recesses. Deep calls unto deep. As you obey and follow My lead, My waves will crash through your being with a resounding **Yes, yes, yes, this is the Way! Walk ye in it!**

West Gardiner, Maine—Blizzard

Gusts of white swirl and fly over the frozen land. Tree limbs are blown and stretched to their limits. Various noises call out in response to the howling winds. Vision is nearly useless in this winter rage. Every living thing has found a hollow in which to burrow, or a shelter in which to wait.

Wait. That is all one can do in this storm. Vision is so limited and conditions are so treacherous. So, I call to you right now, to wait. Yes, the storm is raging now, the elements have collided. All nature has released its fury. There is nothing any human can do in these conditions except wait. It is no different in the unseen realm, My Child. The battle ignites and intensifies to the point where I, and only I must take control of the scene. Alone, you are indeed powerless, but that is alright, because you are not alone. I say to you today, I am your Right Arm and I will deliver you out of this storm and into a paradise such that today's storm will not be a bad memory, but will be a **Song of Triumph** for you. ✔

How is this possible? A better question to ask is, how is this *not* possible with the God of the Impossible on your side? I shall turn this very storm into a Testimony of Victory over the darkness, so others who are going through their storms will not relent. As they hear from you that I am still the God Who is actively parting the Red Sea, they, too, will be able to stand firm to the end. They and you will also be overcomers in My great and marvelous stories that will be heralded for all eternity.

Yes, just as the men and women in My Old Testament accomplished astonishing, naturally impossible feats, so you, too, and countless others, shall be delivered from the snare of the fowler and placed into My glorious and eternal storybook, "Heroes After My Own Heart." All who laid it down for MY namesake, those who counted not the cost of their lives, but *truly* found **Me,** and those who, once tasting of Me, were never able to live for self again! Those precious ones have touched the most delicate places of My heart. This, My Child, is the mark of True Love and True Devotion. These are the ones who will reign with Me in My kingdom forevermore. This storm is the very highlight of your story in this, *My marvelous Book of Honor.*

West Gardiner, Maine—Morning Moon After Blizzard

Amidst a world of colorless white, and the background of a shade somewhere between the babiest of blues and dancing tropical waters, is the *Illuminating Moment of Soul Meeting Me.* Against a platform of mere barren branches, I advance My way into the morning hours. I greet you, this morning, in an all-encompassing, mesmerizing Morning Moon.

I have stood watch through the night, the night after the storm. And I, the ever-present One, wait for our morning connection, reaching outside the world of words and emotional highs. My beauty steadily lifts into the great blue and sinks into all the sky, permeating it with My presence. I herald this morning's greeting to all My creation.

Look outside the walls of your prison locking you away from Me. Look above your monotonous gaze that cannot encompass Me. I am right here, in the vast, blue mass, enveloping you in My embrace.

11

Michigan Messages along Quiet Amish Countryside

Onsted, Michigan, W.J. Hayes State Park

Nothing of spring is in sight. All around, the colors remain brown with missing leaves, yet the day is as warm as the height of spring's embrace. Songbirds

proclaim their excitement as prominently as if the season were truly upon us. Shades of winter's brown contrast deeply with the continuous, melodious sounds of life and warm sun.

The trail ends at a body of water. A dock appears above the idyllic, glassy scene. Two silent masses of brilliant white come into view as the thick spread of trees and bare bushes give way. There they are, floating in perfect peace, a symbol of pure beauty. Uninhibited by human presence, the great swans continue dipping their long necks into the water and basking in the day's spring tease.

It is coming. Can you not perceive it? My songbirds even know the advancing season of life is coming. The signs are around you. While at first glance the scene appears the same dull brown color, nonetheless, I say to you spring truly advances. The season is shifting. Its motion cannot be stopped, for I ordain the changing of seasons. It is by My hand when you see new growth appearing in the dead, lifeless ground. Bright green shoots will emerge and grow into robust, lush lifeforms. Growing as quickly as a dandelion, this tender green rapidly overtakes the ground and becomes deeply rooted and nearly impossible to pull and remove. The bright yellow flower will multiply, overtaking the once-barren ground. So, too, is your spring within moments of erupting, commenced by My spiritual charge.

So aggressive, My power will consume any death in its path, replacing it with multiplication of life. That is My specialty. The cross was the ultimate example of life, magnified and multiplied through excruciating death. *I need no special circumstance to make all things new.* ✓

Tipton, Michigan, Hidden Lake Gardens

It is only the second day of March. These gardens are lovely, no doubt, but it is still too early to see any colors or growth. The hiking trails are all brown, although there is some green in valleys where water has collected. The pond is calm and a pair of Canadian geese can be seen at the edge. The land expands into different collections of gardens and trees. The beauteous and towering evergreen section proudly displays its green, which stands out now, perhaps more than at any other time of year.

The indoor displays of plant life are most impressive. The cactus and tropical vegetation have sustained through the northern winter in their protected domes, where human tending has provided correct temperature and dew point requirements. Safe in their bubble, such tropical life is a wonder to see, when just outside the glass dwelling, winter coldness is still in the air and the sun makes only an occasional appearance.

Coming from the outside and stepping into this tropical world is immediately uplifting. The large rainforest leaves abound in all shades of green, towering above the viewer. The most impressive, most immediate sighting is the breathtaking banana tree, its towering height and massive size seen upon first entrance. Just one of the leaves is the size of a human. Reaching the top of the great dome, the banana tree boasts its mighty height above all the rest. It showcases its masses of bananas hanging in great clumps. Papaya and mango trees are also decorated with their bounty. An orange tree is dotted with tiny, bright fruits. Even a delightful cacao tree and coffee are here. A lemon tree has the most perfect, (are they really real?) largest and gorgeous suspended fruits. The temptation to take one flits through the mind; a piece of this life to take back, yes, that is what one wants. The best alternative to knowing you cannot remain in this world seems to be possessing some of the vibrant beauty. But alas, all must remain as is. Not a blade of anything may be taken, only the sensation and memory of this dome are allowed to depart.

Not so with Me, I am your paradise that goes far beyond an experience. A sensation or memory? Ha! I am the Reality of Life! I create in you an ever-sustaining harvest of fruits able to produce in any climate, in any condition. Yes, My people are My most endowed and extolled creation. They are My most marvelous display of life; the most coveted in the real realm—that of the unseen. When you are engrafted to Me, the only certainty is a constant, abundant life that never dwindles or fades!

West Gardiner, Maine—Evening Pond Declaration

It is a call to Me. Do you have ears to hear the sweet lullaby fashioned from deep within the life of each creature? They are calling to Me, their finest symphonies ringing and echoing across the water and declaring, "Glory and honor to You, Most Magnificent, the Irresistible Embodiment of Utter Satisfaction, fulfilling every chasm of desire that exists in us and leaving no fiber wanting! More, more, more we cry out to You, Almighty One, to be wrapped this evening in Your magnetic presence!"

This is the very cry of My creatures tonight. They know Me and the awe of My presence. Mankind, I have made you higher than all other forms of life on earth. The bellowing bull frogs, chiming crickets, ringing loon, and the slapping beaver tail exude their enthusiastic call to Me. How much more I desire each and every human, My sons and daughters, to cry out with such fervor to be with Me, laying aside all requests and reservations, except: **"More Lord, more, give us more of You!"**

12

Alaska Looming

Waldoboro, Maine—Quiet Bay

Did you think today I miscalculated? Did you think yesterday was an oversite on My part? Was My "to do" list too burdensome? Was I too busy in My gardens? Or did I simply disappear into the mystical space surrounding the Heavens? *Did I forget?*

~Surprises Await~

All those concepts are outside of Me. They do not exist. *I am too great, too unquenchable, too limitless, too brimming and spilling over of pure love, for such things are immediately tidal-waved out to sea before touching Me.* They pretend to be here but only lurk in the dark places in the ocean of the mind, holding on by hands of fear and doubt. But I saturate all things, just as the ocean you see before you saturates everything it touches, and everything it doesn't! Its salt affects all life in and out of the water. But reality is not these dark things, because I say to you today, *reality is Me and Me alone! All those things are the deep illusions on your pathway to eternal life.*

I lead you here, not to labor, My Child, but to be saturated in My choice setting. It is your date with destiny. Enter. The wilderness is behind, the vast ocean of possibilities awaits. You are aligned, mind, body, and spirit. Do not look back!

Continue on your journey. I will lead and guide you. Continue in your newfound stance and confidence of seeking My path! Oh, what surprises lie ahead when you are on My marvelous path of self-denial and growth. Oh, the rewards of those who have pressed on, despite fear, despite the sting of pain and abandonment, with uncertainty flooding in; **My ultimate risk takers!** I give you the highest offer of a life lived to the fullest, because you have yielded to your insatiable, unquenchable thirst that only My leading relieves.

So, scan the ocean waters now. What possibilities lay where you cannot see? It does not matter if you are blind, Child, if you have My leading. Truly, without Me, the eagle's vision is an unfortunate condition, compared to those with complete blackness of physical vision, yet having My leading. Child, since when can you see into the crevices of the deep ocean waters? And do you have the insight to tell where every wave of the ocean will turn and bend and lead? When the storm will subside? Where the rainbow begins? Indeed, I do! The sailing is smooth now. The ocean water is mere lake ripples today, right now. It is safe, it is by My design, that you move into the unknown. It is My delight to walk with you, hand in hand, into all new fertile territory. *The Great Ancient of Days, Lover of your Soul, Father of all Fathers, has your back!* All is quiet; the tide has silently come in at a shocking rate. It is time, time to move swiftly!

13

Alaska & Washington Chime In

Coffman's Cove, Alaska

This land is all by My design, imprinted with My very nature. Rugged and true, standing the test of time, there is the severity of environment, yet the gentle fragrance of tranquility in the air. Everything shouts to all who pass by; I am here! I hold the answers! I am endowed with wisdom surpassing the limits of present time. I see far into the sea and know what path every bend of each ocean wave will take. *Surely, I know your situation.* I am not a God Who abandons or gives second best. No, My blessings have the massive roots of the great hemlock and spruce, affecting all others around you.

Your roots will intertwine with some others, causing immovable support, and unshakeable dreams that give nourishment to awaken dormant life. My breath of life breaks all dormancy and solitude, causing new life to emerge into reality. Quicken those things around you. Call forth that which is dead to come alive. Now is the time to enact My kingdom truths, *My marvelous principles that defy the laws of nature and allow the reality of My very nature to be wrought into another.*

Coffman's Cove, Alaska

Out of the most rugged terrain, where cold salt water contends with tall spiny grasses and an array of jagged ledges and rocks. This is where the water slaps the scattered, whitened logs across the shoreline, only to lay home for the tiny mink, a shelter from which to pop-up and peer. Here is where the bear pads his way across his kingdom of wilderness, where mountain regions expand into thick growths of fir and spruce, where only the finest specimens are most likely to survive.

Here is where I placed and freely scattered domes of of pink and purple bells in every hue, the most delicate shades in the most fragile form. Standing erect, appearing too tall to remain upright, held by some unseen hand, there in the element where only the tough survive, *they dance, the bells dangling and flowing in the wind.* Fairy tale flowers, spinning as if delighted by some mystical secret. Enchanting. Captivating. All the harshness around this one beauty melts into oblivion. The mesmerizing and carefree sway does not demand such attention, but offers an irresistible allure to the viewer.

Follow Me. Follow Me and love Me with all your heart, soul, and mind. I will take you and, in any circumstance, you will become as the foxglove, no matter what weather, predator, or environment is present.

Coffman's Cove, Alaska—View of Ocean on Rocks

Towering blue mountains lie silent behind the massive stretch of the ocean's kingdom. Great spews of water burst into the air, emitting the deep, breathlike sound into the distance; the great tail slides back into the gentle movement of waves.

Misshapen and freely flowing branches parallel the shoreline, giving way to the jagged cliff bordering the waters. Eagles fly over the expanse. A raven sends out his cackly call. "Awaken, awaken, from your slumber all who have an ear to hear. All you see here will disappear. For I, The Great Master of Time, am turning the sands of time into extinction."

Awaken My soldiers! Arise My warriors! Time is a most precious commodity I have given you. How grief stricken the hearts of man will be on that day when I look into their faces and ask, "What is your account of the gift of time I allotted you? Where is the increase that stems into eternity? No, Mankind, your vacations, possessions, and pampering of the flesh, when cashed in here, only bring you into bankruptcy. Things here are never as they are perceived on earth.

Show Me the kindness endowed in My name. Reiterate the times of life you bestowed upon the weary traveler, tell Me your seeking to lead another, your times of prayer for lost and dying souls. How many others are here, oh man, because of My passion burning through you, giving the gift of eternal life to another? What is the eternal value of your time on earth when presented here?"

Today, the moaning seabirds call to those who have ears, "Awaken from your slumber, now, before the window of time itself is sealed forever!"

Wenatchee, Washington—Valley City: View from Ascending Plane

~*For Such a Time as This*~

It is My finger that molded and drew each peak and valley into this part of the earth. So, it is with your life. I line the perimeters of the wilderness, and I also part the Red Sea. Your valley/wilderness is behind. Past is the dusty, barren, red earth. Now, the vast, lush, green forest is here; there is plenty of water to sustain such growth. And grow you have, My Child, through all the traversing in the wilderness. Enter in. Canaan is here. Look at the life, the peaks of dense green.

So is your life about to bring forth such an oasis of outpouring that you can handle now, that you can now spill My love into others, just as it is meant. My genuine gifts touch and spill over into the lives of those around you. They are never meant to be contained. As I endow your life to the fullest, then you easily, effortlessly, naturally ignite the gift of life into others. My most prized, lavishing gift is eternity with Me. Face to face. It is a relationship of which mankind has never conceived, a relationship that bursts crisp air into the lungs, a heartbeat that skips in joy. Ha, Ha,

Yes! It is truly a deep manifestation of joy unspeakable.

Yes, My Child, that's the relationship with Me, beyond feeling and emotion. I am life to the fullest in every cell, changing your barometer from mediocre to truth and reality of life enmeshed in Me! *The barren wilderness is behind. Enter into My vast, lush Canaan land!*

14

Mostly Mid-Coast Maine with a Midwest Interlude

Lisbon, Maine, Androscoggin River Walk

A whitewash floods down upon the state in true northern celebration of Christmas Day. Every crevice is presented with the beautiful covering of pure white. All is silent outside, except for the wind swirling and scattering the dancing snowflakes. Nature sighs in contentment, not dread, of the beautiful gift of solitude. Connected to the Source of this reprieve are the massive evergreens, the hidden creatures, and all that lies below the new blanket of white. This silent day brings with it the greatest gift on Christmas Day.

My gift to you is the silence. It is the solitude. It is Me laid out. Ask of Me, inquire of Me, present to Me the deepest and most sacred places in your heart, those lying beneath the markers of past dreams, nearly **but never** detached from your soul. Ask of Me the buried desires that remain as burning coals, **never completely extinguished**. These places, however, are not meant to ache; instead, they are to bring vitality flowing into your being. Child, these places are not dead ends, *because you are connected to the One who is a Master at igniting dormant dreams and the relentless passions in the human soul.*

These things in you I desire even more, because I placed them there. They are irrevocable parts of your bloodline, a bloodline which, of course, we share. They are most sacred and without replica. *They are unique to each individual and only reside in human beings amidst all My creations.* I love you for them. I envision you walking in them and bestowing the side effects on others to effortlessly heal and restore those around you. In turn, they will be strengthened and enlightened to walk in their ordained passions, creating a mighty host of My brilliant, awe-inspiring human race, no longer in despair and heavily trodden. They will be endowed with My power, My beauty, My essence oozing from their every fingerprint on the earth! Heaven raining down its whitewashing purity and hope will be the result as they journey along this chapter of their life on earth.

This, My Child, is the manifestation of heaven on earth, the result of their intimacy with Me. This is

119

their true destiny on earth, leading them to the un-paralleled joy and never-ending satisfaction: *These actively fulfilled passions are proof indeed that they are on their narrow path, that illusive concept so un-appealing and misunderstood by many on earth; it ushers them to the very gates of My coveted and marvelous, eternal Kingdom!*

Freeport, Maine—Morning Lakeside Hike: Silhouette of the Creator

A frozen February morning awakens and greets the Creator down the crusty, frosty trail. The world with all its cares and sorrows is immediately left behind, *giving way to the other realm, the unseen realm suddenly making an appearance.* The evergreens enclose the white trail. Birds ring out gleeful melodies. The sun, though not really felt in the midst of the cold, brings an understanding that the atmosphere has changed. The woods give way, leading to the lakeside. The sun boasts a powerful luster over the entire scene. *It is the Silhouette of the Creator.* Visible rays from

His dazzling presence stream down through the white clouds, causing the scene to respond from frozen and unchanged, to a voracious frequency of life *doused by His touch.*

It is I, My presence, that has the magnetic ability to transform anything seemingly paralyzed and frozen, into a fresh breath of life. Ha, Ha! Can you picture when I come into the dead scene? No, you can't, until you experience Me! Nothing else can be likened to My endless flow, My reigning Kingdom, **My bottomless, unwalled, yes, ceiling-free expanse of Love.** True contact with Me brings change into the dead carcass. It springs up, abounding in color, laughter, and sheer delight. When you respond, not merely include, and make Me your life, I shine over you, re-writing the dead storyline that erases all of Murphy's Law, and establishing My creative ones.

My creativity exceeds the need for a physical pen, paper, canvas, or instrument, *for truly I need nothing to create your stunning earth story.* I will create all of this for you as you yield and present Me your All, no holds barred. I will ensure you reign in this life; more importantly, nothing will be able to take away the fact that you loved Me enough to give Me your life, the highest evidence of true love. The ultimate accolade of Heaven will be given to those who know Me. Your works will not be celebrated, but **your heart will be,** with **the evidence** of your life spilling over into divine connection with Me!

St. Louis, Missouri—Midwest Thunderstorm

In an instant, the limbs of the massive oak tree bend in response to The Stirring. The Stirring ignites, rushing onto the world below. Blades of grass dance and sway in all directions. Leaves are flying in response to the great Stirring. No creature is in sight; all have noticed and taken shelter. *And the momentum is yet to be harnessed by anyone.*

Indeed, I have seen and I have heard! It is I, the Great and Mighty Stirring. With a domino effect, the earth below responds to My presence. I am moving in the situations of My people as tangibly as this Midwest storm. A meeting of My cool air from the heavens evaporates the heavy and oppressive heat. *I am enmeshed in the hearts of My people.* I have experienced every teardrop that has rolled down your faces in the midnight hour. I have heard the deep, mourning sigh from your innermost depths, and the despair from heated conditions. I send My cooling rain from the ultimate authority, My very throne room, cancelling out the fiery afflictions. Beloved, know, I am The Stirring! I am moving; it is not that I will stir, or I will move, but I am now stirring all things into alignment! A great master view I have and am implementing **now** for you. My Dear Ones, dry your eyes and square your shoulders, for I am stirring and re-creating the scene into such a new picture that you shall feel the breath in your lungs freeze, as your eyes behold My magnificent infusion of Life into that which was dead!

Wolf's Neck State Park - Freeport, Maine

My voice is in every detail this evening. My soul, My very Being, both **tangible,** can be felt in every movement here. My Spirit is hovering. I encapsulate this spot on earth. Did you think it was merely the beauty that led you here tonight? No, I was that deep desire in the innermost recesses of your soul. *I drew you*

here tonight. My pull comes down in a heavy blanket, saturating you and inviting you to commune *face to face* with Me. The seemingly mystical feel here is My weighty presence. The tall spread of bright green ferns in the trail is My Holy Spirit dancing, beckoning you to follow Me off the trail and into Freedom's path. *The alluring sway enlightens the mind, breaking down the barriers of this natural world.*

Such a delight is experienced nowhere else but in Me! The soft waves rocking back and forth over the ledgey coastline are My lullaby, My gift of peace. I dissolve all your cares with My sweet and oh-so-pronounced scent of evergreens; I renew your being with My doses of salty breeze. The path is visibly full of My determined Maine roots sprawling over the ground, supporting your every movement.

Give into My support and nourishment and I will never allow the bitter blows of life to overcome you. My deep roots will sustain you with such hope that nothing in this transient world will be able to destroy you. *Because the Love between us is stronger than any force, more triumphant than any vicious assault of the enemy.* Our Love overrides every obstacle or onslaught of deception seeking to ravage the mind. *You see, My dear One, My Love is so perfect that fear itself is obliterated in our embrace.*

Bristol, Maine, La Verna Land Preserve

I am raw, I am untamed. My ways are as untouchable as the land you see here. I exceed all human thoughts and plans. I go beyond circumstances and break through all jagged places that seek to hold you hostage in this life. The great Atlantic waters rush over seaweed-covered ledges. A massive rocky coastline follows along a stretch of tenacious trees, abounding spiny grasses, and other thriving plant life. Unaccommodating great masses of rock protrude upwards and in various directions.

Here you must pause and decide how, and even if, you will attempt to maneuver the formations. *But I am the original Way-Maker.* My abilities of accessing the new way are so much greater than any formation you see as a barrier. My focus is never concerned with the course ahead. I have no obstacles. My concern is your heart in connection with Mine. This happens as we traverse the world together, leaving behind the stresses of how, and simply being in the journey together. I will make the path clear. Your only concern should be staying close with Me. The more connected you are to Me, the more your soul is enlightened to the reality of relationship with Me. It is like no other.

I never leave, I never abandon, I never forsake or forget. My concern is always your well-being. There is no point at which I leave you behind, not for sleep nor duty. I am a Friend like no other, a Lover who never disappoints. My love is raw and untamed. My love is the deepest, most fulfilling desire in the soul of every human. I know, because I am the One who tailored the place in each heart, that only I should fit. I made it out of My desire for the deepest form of intimacy, reserved only for My matchless passion for you.

Vassalboro, Maine, Webber Pond

The Canadian geese glide along the waters in happy unison. A great reprieve is the pond in the peak of summer's full reign. Not a honk is heard; the presence of the geese is only made known by sight.

It is the highest form of communication. No voice is needed. Such is the look of knowing between two soulmates, the same thought at the exact moment, shared by the best of friends, the bond of understanding that twins share. This is the way of communication in My Kingdom, a deep, innermost assurance. The closer each saint in My kingdom draws to Me, the more this flow is turned on, resulting in a mighty interlocking of unison among My people. This is just one of the spiraling, tell-tale signs of those who are continually interacting with Me. Yes, flowing to life in the fullest is the only way I flow in all areas. I am Life to the Fullest and anything without Me is **always** lacking.

West Gardiner, Maine—Thunderstorm

Without notice, without warning, a crashing explosion dominates the region, highlighted by a charge of illumination. Nothing was revealed to announce its arrival. The storm debuts in full fury, without introduction. A rippling effect charges throughout the atmosphere. The air carries an energy that nothing can resist. The silent trees are suddenly pulsating and swirling in their newfound life. Raindrops plunge to earth, followed by intense sheets of liquid. The waters on the pond now wave in response.

Do you think I need a human welcome to come onto the scene? Do you think I require a sunny, balmy beach day? Do you think My presence needs a captive audience? Or do you know I need nothing to rain down My glory?

Did I need a helping hand or a brainstorming session on how to mold the heavens and the earth? Did I need to gasp for air when I blew light into existence from My breath? Did I need to inquire of some mystical being to help Me evolve a pile of dust into a living likeness of Myself? Or perhaps I needed a blueprint to create something out of nothing?

How utterly useless are these types of measures to Me. My capacity to create, to love, to simply be, is nothing short of I AM. I AM all there is of reality. Anything outside of Me is simply an illusion. I am the Master at creating dead scenes to light up with My all-consuming energy *in an instant*. In fact, should I not give the command to slow My storming atmosphere, all would eventually light up with such fervor that the area could never contain any other thought or coursing of life, except that which drips from My liquid presence. Why do you think the four beasts covered in eyes in Revelation can only exclaim, "Holy, holy, holy, Lord God Almighty, which was, and is, and is to come **for eternity**?" (Revelation 4:8) It is because they are awed by all their eyes as they continually see a new, awesome attribute of Me! Not for a month, nor for a year, but forever, they can never come to the end of seeing all My glory! There is no

127

barrier I can't conquer, nor any wasteland too barren when I thunder onto the scene.

Stockton Springs, Maine—Sandy Point Beach

A beach not well known, and certainly not a top destination for tourists, lies dotted along the massive stretch of rugged Maine coastline. A few locals find their way here today, but most are involved in other endeavors as August nears its end. Dogs are allowed to trot along the shoreline. No lifeguards are present here. It is a relaxed place of freedom. Piles of seaweed abound. The water is clear and cold, but as warm as it will ever be. Seagulls and other sea birds send out their calls. A hawk screeches her warning as one nears her massive nest. The sun's warm rays are perfectly complimented by cloudy breaks of coolness. The sand beckons one with its warmth. The salty water glides in as a sweet lullaby. A trail system in the woods turns into a pleasant little thicket that gives shade to the hiker.

A new trail is connected to this one, the Amazon Trail. At first, it is interesting, but one can soon see why it bears this name. Much of the trail has wooden foot bridges. It is a wet area, somewhat marshy. In fact, it resembles the Amazon in a peculiar way of its own. The trail gets tiring and one can decide it is not very alluring, but it does lead to a shoreline trail. Alas, the shoreline is thicker in vegetation and unkempt. It is a disappointing spot, very mucky and marshy, and the trail along the shoreline seems too overgrown to bother with. The same way back is taken once again, through the Amazon-like terrain. But the way back is seemingly shorter. And the view heading into the pleasant thicket trail is very welcoming. Going out of the trail is not the same as entering. The view is different and there is anticipation of the backdrop view of the beach just in sight.

"Been there, done that." Is that your thought? Is that your perception now? Not with Me on the trail of life! I can take you down the same trail you have trodden a hundred times, even every day of your life, and cause that trail to gush forth a new scene. Be expecting that which I have called from the very graveyard to leap with such an explosion that it is only attributed to My unseen hand.

Missouri—Katy Trail

The trail is massive and stretches across a large geographical area. Today is only a glimpse, a short section of this historical ground. It is just that, history for you. The trail completely surrounds you today. Upward slopes of rock rise far to the right and a sluggish Missouri river is to the left. The thick forest feels very much like a jungle with the high humidity and massive vines encapsulating all about. In fact, in parts of this forest the overhead is completely interlocked around you. I know it feels like a different world than what you are used to. *My Child, I have other intentions for you.* I am leading you out of this area. It is not where I have designed you to flourish. I call you back to your heartbeat, to that place which is a new physical location to you, but a deep soul tie nonetheless! *It is that which is bound to your very DNA.*

How you will get there and how your needs will be met are not in your plans, but in Mine! Your plans and attempts will be futile, but not so with Mine! **I have your back**! In the last seconds, in the last, remaining midnight hour, I will make a way where there is no way! Others could get lost there and fall to the side; it is not their rightful domain on earth. But you, My Child, *this is where you come alive in Me!* This is where you will know Me like no other! I will reveal My face to you in this season of your life. You will never be the same, our relationship will flow out of you as your very breath. Yes! It will be that natural! You will be awakened by Me, transformed in your mind, and heightened to such a perception that old things fall away as I overtake the lenses of your eyes. Feel the beating of My heart and the touch of My hand in this place on earth, *for I have always known I would reveal Myself to you here*, in the most profound, out-of-the-box ways. Be prepared, My Child, you will never be the same as we enmesh into one!

Vassalboro Maine - Togus Pond

Drops of rain form a gentle morning melody onto the world. It is silent except for the soul-satisfying patter. A cool and clean draft lingers from the cracked window. It is too late in the season to be open, but the purity and refreshment it brings is well worth the cool room. The daytime hours are doused in a liquid reprieve. The world seems to have slowed. A rainy Saturday causes many to linger in the comforts of home. Later, in the time between afternoon light and evening darkness, a sudden tidal wave of wind grasps all in sight. Trees bend to the max. One bends beyond its capability, its roots rip up along the water's bank, and the tree now hangs horizontally. It holds on desperately, but the wind is too much; it uproots the tree completely and it crashes to the ground. It causes no damage to anything around it and finally breaks after one last attempt to remain upright. It cannot remain upright. The mighty wind overpowers and rips back the deep roots.

I am cutting off the formerly unmovable roots in one swipe! Yes, in one moment, I call forth a breaking off of past ties that have held My people. You have sustained uprightness through many raging storms and I have watched by your side. The roots have tried to remain in My windstorm, but they could not, because I have not allowed them to. It is I you have seen in the mighty windstorm tonight! I have not just cut you off from these ties, but I have completely demolished them at the roots! They will now dry up and die. Once they held onto you with a captive grip, but now they are becoming powerless stubble.

These very roots, once so oppressive to you, will transform and become the fertilizer for your new ground. You shall rise above them full of vigor and utilize those things that once tried mercilessly to pin you to the grave! They shall now evoke great laughter from your innermost being, a laughter of triumph for you and for those who shall feast off this fertilizer, this infusion of life from that which was dead.

This is the same indwelling, life-transforming power that came from My very death on the cross. Relax in a sweet place, such as a peaceful rainy morning of rest, as I build the momentum that will uproot you and place you into My Divine design. Understand, My dear One, when I do the uprooting, the new ground in which I place you will be charged with My current. It will electrify your new roots into a massive display of foliage.

15

Words of the Southwest

Albuquerque, New Mexico - Sandia foothills

It is January here in this world that hardly breathes a winter's trace. Today, the sun is warm and the day feels of spring. On the trail, a tiny roadrunner dashes by. Cacti pepper the rocky terrain. The mountains in the distance are in stark contrast to the immediate ones. The snow spreads across the background, yet those closest are perfectly bare of any white.

The terrain has been difficult, My Child. It has gone on and on. The way has seemed parched; no water has been seen near or distant. Only your faith in My character has allowed one foot to pass the other. The conditions have played with your mind as a desert mirage, but these mirages have been your hope, your faith, expecting to see the conditions change. You have been hoping for the breakthrough, again and again. This continual fixation has kept you going, rather than destroying you. The merciless heated conditions have all but displayed their haughty arrogance to suppress and kill the dreams I have placed in every one of My children.

Today, various trails along these foothills can be taken, but there is only one precise way for *each* of My children. *For you see, dear One, I shine the way amidst all the ways in which you could go from here. Now I give the command for all to be straightened; your situation, mistakes, and obstacles are immediately hurdled away from your life as you take My leading. All that remains is My highest calling for you on this path! Truly getting here is the toughest trail, it is the ancient path. It is the most exceedingly narrow, unfamiliar, and solitary hike of one's life, generally wrought with many heart-wrenching falls from the harsh conditions. Understand that every one of these falls you have taken has been felt as deeply in My own heart. My Beloved, you may have seen them as your failures, but to Me they have decorated you as a tried-and-true veteran of honor, because My love for you is greater than any devastating fall. I am your Prize, Child, and I am assuredly worth all the victories and all the losses, for I am the Ultimate Attainment in Life.*

New Mexico, Jamez Mountains

The silence here is divine. It is living life with the ceasing of all works, all striving, the release of every strain. *This is living with Me in the present moment, not the past or future, but right now. This is how I have designed you to be.*

The rugged and dark striped bark of the pines extends into the sky; green needles give release to the gentle drift of air. The massive mountains surround the scene in their white coating of winter's remaining touch. A gentle lullaby of spring's welcome is heard on and off. The air is cool and freshly intoxicating.

Did I not say your burden will be light and your yoke easy? I do not change, no matter your surroundings or the current opinions of society. There is no need to pick up your burden once you leave this beautiful place. *I will carry your burden.* It has always belonged with Me, dear One. My brutal road to the cross led to your most beautiful gift, the gift of true love, always wrapped in truth. Any striving to carry your load is merely the flesh laboring. *It is not your act of true love to Me.* It becomes an act of true love towards Me when your innermost overflows denial of self with eagerness to please Me, showing Me your undying gratitude. It is not and never will be about your good intentions or humanistic deeds, as is so prevalently displayed in today's culture of false love. These acts are always pointed directly back at self. They are always soothing to the flesh, bringing the false belief systems of good works over My transforming grace.

Faith in Me **personally** is what brings the change of destiny to you and brings abundant life into your every fiber. No belief system on earth, nor any religion of man, could ever produce this, My gift of pardon. I am the Truth. It is not a state of enlighenment. It is I, it is Who I am. Anything else is deception, and on the day of accounting, will leave you stripped. Explanations and reasonings will cease in the presence of My Spirit of Truth on that day.

My Beloved, please take heed now, while you still have the power to choose eternity with Me, *My greatest desire.* Faith in Me, Jesus Christ of Nazareth, will release to you this eternal life secured by Me, Faithful and True, and My all conquering love. My dear One, the transitory state in which you live now, and your current understanding, make it impossible to grasp what is in store for those who have chosen Me. The real life is that which is to come, My abundant and sovereign kingdom. It is all magnetized by My presence, leaping with life brimming over, as My smile immerses the atomsphere in **pure, true love,** *My very likeness!*

I am the only manifestation of true love! Anyone who believes in Me knows true love and is forever on the pathway of the ceasing of works and reasonings. They effortlessly overflow My relationship with them and love others in truth! Their eyes now open, they desire all to come into alignment. No longer are they able to sell the truth for the lies pervading this present society. These lies will never be able to reside in them again. Once they have taken My hand and accepted Me as the Way, the Only Way, they are never able to settle for the lies again within themselves, nor sell them to anyone else. Once one has tasted Me, the Truth, he can never again settle for any other.

16

Deep Calls unto Deep; Messages of the Atlantic

Washington, Maine, woods - Coronavirus Time

Those who seek Me, *find Me*. My peace will be the marker of them in the turbulent hour upon the earth. There are ones who have sought after Me, even in the times of ease. Others have gone great physical distances to find Me. *And I admonish them so.* Some have given up every safety net, every material thing, just to see My face. *Such love courses through My being for them.* Some have walked the desolate, solitary desert road to hear My voice. *How I delight in speaking personally to each one.* Some have watched from dawn to dusk each day, searching the sky for My coming. *The anticipation of our union is the highlight I eagerly await.*

I am the **only** Prize to be found in a mansion adorned in jewels, just as I am the only Prize to be found in the empty prison cell. Your manner and circumstance never change your need for Me. The wealthy elite are in no way less needy of me than the homeless addict. The life that has been ripped apart, and the life of luxury and ease, are both in desperate need of relationship with Me! You see, My Child, your status and lifestyle have made you neither less nor more in need of My salvation.

Your perception and desire for Me should not change in your given circumstance. Eternity and My love do not hinge on these factors. You can be living the humblest, most despised existence on earth, and yet you are bound for My celestial kingdom! Nothing, nothing can ever rob you of that, lest you make the choice to walk away from Me. The position in which you see a person might be considered an embarrassment, even a failure, from man's perspective. Yet, you do not know that I have called the one to this labor, I have created them to withstand society's pressure without swaying. *Only I have seen their heart, their love for Me, despite seeming to have been passed over.*

The faithfulness to Me, and life given to those they encounter, is one of the highest accolades in My kingdom: To be a true servant to a lost and dying world. Those who are viewed lowest in My kingdom are the haughty and arrogant of heart. Their own worldly success has corrupted their minds into thinking they have no need to acknowledge their Creator.

Into the woods you went today, searching for one of My blessings of health I have given the earth. Man is in a state of panic and fear now, watching the headlines and turning to other means to save them. How I wish they would stop. Listen to My songbirds. They are at peace, singing My love over the land.

If they would only listen to the message. I have all the answers that man's solutions could never give you! I bid each one to come and **ask**. I will fulfill your needs as they come into play. After searching high and low on your hike today, you found My gift of health in the current wave of fear upon the earth. Those who seek Me, find Me. I give to you what you need. Come away with Me and find the cure to **every** illness or condition known to man. I am greater than any circumstance, and *I so delight in shining the way.*

Rockport, Maine - Aldamere Shoreline Trail

The trail was a surprise today. You were not looking for it in particular, but there was the tiny opening in the trees. *I knew you'd be by here today, even though you didn't. I have been waiting for you, and I have enlightened the way.* Nobody is on the trail today. The evening is coming and the recent spring snowstorm created such a fury that people are locked in their houses, locked at home with no power. The electrical current has been cut off to these homes, just as My electrical current has been cut off in their lives. *Powerless.* This is no condition to be in during these turbulent times. My heart grieves for those who are not cognizant of Me. *How I want to help them. How I want to show them the only true way in the mazes of their lives.*

The trail soon goes downhill. It is slippery from the storm with snow, puddles, and mud. The forest lay in silence as the evening invades. A way down to the rocky shoreline is available, but not terribly easy. *The way can be very difficult at times, My Beloved.* It could even break you, if you are not in My firm grasp.

I have seen many of My beloved people fall prey to vicious attacks, their minds shattered, hearts bleeding, the circumstances too terrible for anyone without Me. But you are in My grasp, in a hand-lock so tight that no power on earth or below could ever pull us apart. The shoreline is empty. It is ours this evening. The mighty Atlantic sprawls out its majestic display. It is quiet tonight, with only a few small islands to be seen. Seagulls are quiet in the Master's presence. *I am the unceasing lullaby to all who stop and make their abode with Me.*

Back up the thickly-wooded, wet trail, the desire to stay along the coastline still resonates. So, a walk along the quiet road is taken to be able to see the great view from the nearby spot ahead. Suddenly, attention turns to the woods next to the road. Not a noise has been made, but a greyish coat can be seen.

Then, instantly, eye-to-eye, the gaze locks. Giant, round, permeating dark eyes stare into mine. I stare back. The connecting gaze is above that of which an animal seems capable. The deer is 10 feet away. We stay in each other's sight. Moments pass. Amazingly, the animal stays mesmerized, glued to me. All else blurs into nothingness. This is what happens when you gaze into My eyes. *Nothing else matters.* The surrounding circumstances melt and the intent look in My eyes is as a magnet for yours.

Nothing could ever pull us apart. We exist as one. No words are even necessary. It is complete understanding; it is genuine trust, an igniting explosion of love that never fades. My Dear One, when faced with My gaze, not a soul would choose any other way. Nothing could ever be so appealing. I am the Way, the Truth, and the Life. *I am your Faithful and True forevermore. Come away with Me and you will never be lost or wanting again; for those conditions are impossible with Me. But instead, when in My gaze, I become the Key to unlocking the identity in which you were created. Those who are eye-to-eye with Me have only one outcome, to win the earthly race and My finest eternal destiny.*

Owl's Head, Maine, Ash Point

An alluring, mossy-lined New England rock wall beckons those on the path to step inside its storybook land. *Come see My mysteries revealed here.* The opening in the rock wall leads to a trail with thick, robust roots sprawling across the path. The coastal trees stand in silence, rugged and impressive from their time on this beautiful yet harsh environment. Clean, crisp air is evident as the usnea hanging from the trees, nicknamed "Old Man's Beard." *It is as if My face is in the glory of these trees and My very breath cleansing away all that could pollute.* The enticing land leads the hiker to a deep admiration and love, as if an intersecting of matching DNA is present. *A sharing of DNA is indeed here, My Beautiful One. You are a repilca of My DNA, Yes, Death-Never-Again. The irresistible attraction in this place is Me. The atmosphere is lit and spilling over in reciprocated love. My energy in this place douses everything as thoroughly as the salt.*

The trail gives way to rugged rocks over the sprawling mass of Atlantic Ocean. An island in the distance is lined with evergreens as tall and straight as proud soliders guarding their land. Below a deep churning and gurgling thunder can be heard rushing in and out of the seaweed-covered crevices. A seagull takes no notice as he meanders above the powerful waves. Gently, he simply soars by in full confidence, without hesitation or concern. *It is because My hand guides all of My creation. I have not walked away from one creature. My compassion is so great and My love so uncontainable, I guide even the seagull you see now. His confidence is evident because he is not relying on his own knowledge and strength. He is in My palm.*

For surely it is never by your might, never by your own power, but by My Spirit that makes the way. I created the flailing sea you watch today, and I tell you I am surely in control of it. Nothing is too dangerous, no obstacle too big with Me. When tied to Me, you are destined to be the superhero of the battle; though battered at times, we always win in the end. Losing is not in our DNA, My Child. DNA: Death Never Again. We are life, no matter what conditions are on earth. The earth I created has no power over us together. I am the Supreme Authority over all things in Heaven and on earth. And your rightful place, My Precious One, is hand-in-hand with Me.

*Never forget, nothing can defeat you because My ferocious love can never be satisfied. It can never peak. It can never lose interest. My steadfast grip will never release. Lovely One, **never** can I lose My connection to you; we are one, always and forevermore.*

Washington, Maine – Rainbow Appears

I love you. I love you. I open the Heavens in this moment and splash a brilliant likeness of Myself

142

directly into your life. A huge, perfect semi-circle hangs from the sky, encasing an entire corner of field. The colors dazzle the half-rainy sky. The solemn, cloudy field has now become a portal for new dimensions. Possibilities, possibilities, My children! What do you think is possible when I enlighten the scene from grayscale to brilliant colors of high dimension? Surely what happens with Me is that you go from your mundane, dull, cloudy sight to vision. Sight is a shadow of dullness, albeit the earthly condition; vision is reality of life in full color of Me. My colors bring to life all that comes into contact with Me. I am the Breath of Life, My Child, so latch onto Me. You will never again see through the old dull lens, when walking in My kalediscope of dimensions.

Washington, Maine – Sea Air

What were you expecting today as you came out of your domain and stepped into ours? Everyday you meander outside your home in the morning hours and enjoy My fresh air and cool breeze. Today I rush to meet you; immediately, your expectations and familiarity with the scene vanish. I can and do change any scene at any moment. In fact, I don't need your help, your anguish, good behavior, or even repentance before I make a move.

Did I need any of these things from you before I carried the cross and walked that solo path for you? Did I need your repentance first? Your skills? Or even a guarantee of your dedication to me? No, My Child, none of these did I require. My love was the only driving force, as it is today! Be free in this knowledge. Watch as I accomplish what no man or plan could ever do. Today, I rush My entire being into you, encompassing everything you are with My fresh salty air!

Although you are not on the coastline today, I have no problem reaching you and giving a fresh salty dose to preserve and uphold not only you, but the dear ones you will encounter along our path together. Breathe deeply and know that I am here. I am in you to embody you, and be one. Your mind will be as Mine. We are conforming and enmeshing together. Our thoughts will be on a plane far higher than simple "like minds." It will be a connection so superior that we will not be two, but one entity, as a marriage solidified in blood, and higher than mere human blood with My Spirit pulsating through the covenant.

So I promise you that the saying, "till death do us part," has no meaning in our relationship. My blood goes higher and further and deeper than any perceived limitation. Death has no power over our covenant. My Precious One, when I proclaimed, "It is finsihed," I covered all bases. I am more than just truthful, I am Truth! I am the Way! *We are life **together** forevermore.*

Bristol, Maine - Laverna Preserve

Wintergreen, bright mosses, and lush green ferns cover the ground today. The evergreens reach into the sky, their heights hidden, towering upward into the foggy mass. An opening from the limbs above showcases a thick, bright white. Its contrast to the forest is beckoning and, though silent, it can be heard.

It is My invitation that is dripping, giving a taste, and moistening the atmosphere. *I am the Mist.* Though silent to the fleshly ear, it is undeniable to those who have an ear to hear My Spirit. Come, come into this realm with Me. You must look up from all attempts to stumble you in the path. Only then will your feet become weightless and you will loosen from the natural restraints. Look up, gaze into My brilliant whiteness above. I am inviting you, calling you. Yes, indeed, there is realm upon realm to walk together hand-in-hand. My kingdom is not of this world. I have called you out of this world and into the realms that wait and burst with new buds in anticipation of My sons and daughters.

Washington, Maine

There is nothing that can overshadow My thick presence of love when I hear My people communing with Me in the morning hours. I have been here all along, through every tick of the clock in the darkness of night. As you rise once again, I hear you calling My name, *and I embellish your view.* Bold columns of rays stream downward from the clouds to the grass. I am illuminating Myself as glowing stripes through the dense fog over the field. You cannot see through the fog, yet it is powerless to hide Me. This brilliant view of Me burns down through the clouds and endows everything below with My light and love. All creation celebrates the ending of night and dawning of morning. Just as the night recedes and loses its power in My advancing presence, so all chains unlock over you. A simple call to Me in the morning activates the signal, stirring all of Me, drawing Me. *If you listen closely, you will hear Me advance. If you look with the eyes of your heart, you will see Me.*

New Harbor, Maine, Saltwater Pond Preserve

A beautiful, quiet salt pond lay in repose as much as the continuous stirring of untamed waves in the ocean beyond. The little pond is amidst piles of rocks and seaweed. In the broad view of the wild Atlantic, throwing surges of waves can be seen only feet away. It is an astonishing mass of brilliant blue. Rocks of many sizes and shapes lead up to the tantalizing, crystal-clear salt pond. Interesting forms can easily be seen on the bottom. The top is smooth, no ripples detected. A divider of rock and seaweed splits the contrast of the two bodies of water.

My offer to you in this time of upheaval is to immerse in My quiet salty pond. You must immerse to dwell with Me in My secret place. So, I say to you now, break away from the wave of fear across the earth today, and free yourself from all that would engulf you now. There is no danger here, My Love, for it is the place I created your soul to be! The waters enmesh your form; no part of you remains untouched. It is My highest offer to you, *My Secret Place,* where all else remains outside the boundary, just as you see the churning waves of the sea beyond these quiet waters.

I will take your mind beyond a mere physical place! My Dear One, you will be in tune with a place far beyond what is here on the earth's plane. Though the wild waters can easily be seen in close proximity, you are above the feeble senses of mortal man's mind *because you now have your being with Me. As you live and breathe in My Secret Place, so shall your mind be heightened to new ways of being, with concepts that obliterate your notions of earth's restrictions.* My salt will add the zest needed to taste the New Way. My sunlit water will give an astonishing depth of clarity to your view. You will hear a new sound, the crashing waves beyond will quiet in the midst of My voice. Perception, My Dear, perception, no longer a state of mind, **but enlightenment of the Truth**!

Your gaze on the peaceful pond water is a mirror reflection of Me. It is as Peter walking on the waters and gazing upon Me. Beloved, all you need do is take My hand. Any idea of peace, or feeling of peace, prior to immersing in My pond, will be a mere illusion of the past, as you accept my highest offer in the Secret Place, and make your abode with The Prince of Peace.

Washington, Maine—Intimacy vs Companionship

Companionship. Sweet companionship gives images of two side-by-side in relationship. Companionship can come from any two human beings, friends, co-workers, teammates, and those involved in like interests. It brings a common interest or desire into a moment. Marriages bring an element of companionship. A union between people brings companionship. Even an animal can provide companionship. But there is a higher walk of unity, My Child, where companionship is still a part, but not the whole. Companionship can be pleasant, but there is a far higher walk to live out with another.

Did you hear the morning call of the bird nearby? It is a call to those in this walk. Yes, indeed the walk is so sweet that there is no need or desire for "space apart." Such an idea never enters the mind, for there is no need for replenishment, *as My love fulfills all needs*, whereby this walk ALWAYS lifts the other *effortlessly*. Companionship in its positive form provides joy for an element or time frame. I am not talking about an amount of time shared, an ending or beginning.

My offering to you is a move of the heart beyond a state of emotion or clock. It is **intimacy** in its true form; striving ceases and love continually overflows. The burden of the duty to spend "quality time" ends as our intimacy supersedes all else. Our dance of fervent eye gaze must never end. Eyes locked, heart, mind, and spirit open. No barriers, and all transparency on display, *selfish pride is left outside our glide.* We are One. And as One we live, and move, and have our being together! You are never left alone.

Are you fearful My beloved? If yes, know that I am offering you more than what you are partaking. Perfect love casts out fear! Is peace that passes all understanding and joy unspeakable your constant? If not, then know that these attributes become your very personality with Me! I take care of **all details** while we have the overflow and joy of communion, fellowship, and companionship. Companionship is highly sought-after and lovely indeed, but it is only a slice of what I offer. My depth of relationship with you is far more involved than any pleasure. It is the joining of the two of us into One. All that I Am is not outside you, but within you. And likewise, all that you are melts and molds as intimate love penetrates and transforms you into the new creation. *Oh glorious day when My love collides upon the open heart.*

Liberty, Maine – Lake St. George

It is the sensation of your mind, body, and soul enwrapped with Me today. Every detail you experience here is Me, orchestrating, wooing, hovering. Yes, I know it is pure joy for the physical senses today. The surface of the lake is as smooth and comforting as a hot beverage to the body. The purity of the water is evident; one can easily see to the bottom of the spring-fed lake. Such as I am to you. I am the spring that continually cleans all debris away. I will not allow any pollutant, no matter how miniscule, to invade you, My Beloved. All you need do is rest and I shall do that work. Worries get washed aside as you trust Me and know that it is all under My control. My infilling will pour into you and nothing will be amiss. Nothing is overlooked as you hold fast to the truth of My nature and fling aside any belief that is not of My character. My infilling of spring waters will encompass all of you. The blockages and stagnant areas will be washed, creating a new being. Not merely a cleaned one, My Lovely, but a new being only I can create. Truly this is your birthright and your true self.

I planned out a stunning portrait that this earth life itself tries to steal from you. I did not create you as a copy of anything but Myself! Never allow yourself to be deadened with conformity, for therein you also relinquish your destiny. I placed giftings, callings, and your true personality that only come alive when you are living in My spring-fed flow.

The slate of smooth rock glides down to the open body of water. The sky is a blue which no one other than I am able to create. The shoreline forest showcases streams of light as though stars shine through the great branches of evergreens. But the deeper flow here is what you are sensing with your spirit. Our connection. Can you see what your physical eyes cannot, the shining light of My silhouette? Can you hear My voice, not by way of your physical ear, but in that melodious silence in the air? Did you smell the unmistakable clean aroma of scent lingering in your spirit, my spring-fed water cleansing the atmosphere? Can you feel the wind of My Spirit dancing through you? Today is not an experience, but the way of life with those hidden in Me.

Washington, Maine – Rainstorm and Power Outage

Massive trees dance wildly, succumbing to the throes of the rainstorm. Sheets of rain fling sideways to the ground, succumbing to the force. The wind mercilessly dominates all that can be shaken, the earth below succumbs to its demands as debris shakes, breaks, and scatters. The wind howls in a rage, ordering all to take heed.

But wait. Here in the heavens I sit upon My throne, My ears keenly aware of a sound that is not succumbing. *I can hear it. Yes, there it is indeed, the storm is but a **whisper** in light of this sound!* My heart swells, and **I, the Great I AM, King of all Kings, *am moved.*** I am moved by this sweet melody, which is as captivating to Me as the strings of a master violinist, but more endearing to My heart, piercing to the depths of My soul. I gaze into the earth's specific region from whence I hear this sound. And yes, *I see you, I see all of you!* Pride, compassion, unfailing love radiates all over Me. It is you Beloved, every voice of My children, each one a solo to My ears, praising Me, thanking Me, loving Me! How I race, I race to each one personally for the blessed communion, the face-to-face relationship we share. The storm rages, yet our mutual love is outside it. It has no impact on us, Dear One.

This is the **highest** regard in My kingdom. This is My highest priority. Nothing else will ever compare *to our union.* You see this is the reason for it all! The creation story, the garden, Satan's malevolent obsession, mankind's fall, My death, My resurrection, and all of the story that is yet to come in the future. My Beloved, the love between us is the very reason for it all. The story of mankind, the plot, is whether you fully accept My offer or not. That is it. There is no reason for this existence except *to be with Me **fully**, every part of you leaping and saying yes!* I make all the rest happen, My Lovely! Yes, your hand in My hand, your face to My face is the answer for it all! *Relationship with Me is the very purpose for the story of mankind.*

Washington, Maine

The coming evening portrays nothing but peace as songbirds chime and the crickets chirp to signal the day's end. Pure beauty is displayed as the evergreens reach high into the sky, their soft green barely moving from the gentle air. The grasses have been washed in a rain for the last few days and shimmer once again. Gone are the dust and pollen. The grey rain clouds are exiting the scene and making way for tomorrow's sunny debut.

So My debut is also coming swiftly, My Child. The evening darkness is upon the world, and it will surely gain in intensity until a full-blown blackness has settled. *But you do know* **the inevitable morning sun is just around the corner, too!**

In a matter of hours the scene will totally change. I, too, am just around the corner. As the seconds tick away, the light becomes greater until in the final second, that one instant, when the morning appears in fullness. I am your Morning Light, yes, your Bright Morning Star, and will snatch all My beautiful ones away with Me forevermore.

Never again will you know pain, nor will teardrops wet your face. Fear will cease to ever enter your mind. Once I gather you, My Cherished Ones, in this moment your destiny begins! *Utter fulfillment, satisfaction surpassing every cell and every facet;* ***this will be our union***. Take heart, My Dear Ones, for I am thundering through the atmosphere to rescue you. Listen, listen closely, and in the distance you will hear the mighty hooves pounding beneath Me, the unbridled cry of My stallion advancing. No power, no supernatural being, no earthly kingdom, NOTHING

153

will stop Me *in My quest for you.* Be ready, be ever listening, for My arrival is unstoppable.

Cobbosee Lake, Maine

Edgecomb, Maine

ABOUT
KHARIS PUBLISHING

KHARIS PUBLISHING is an independent, traditional publishing house with a core mission to publish impactful books, and channel proceeds into establishing mini-libraries or resource centers for orphanages in developing countries, so these kids will learn to read, dream, and grow. Every time you purchase a book from Kharis Publishing or partner as an author, you are helping give these kids an amazing opportunity to read, dream, and grow. Kharis Publishing is an imprint of Kharis Media LLC. Learn more at https://www.kharispublishing.com.